...by the dawn's early light

...the twilight's last gleaming

...through the perilous fight

...were so gallantly streaming

...are, the bomb bursting in air

...ight that our flag was still there

...banner yet wave

...the home of the brave?

...through the mists of the deep

...host in dread silence reposes

...eze, o'er the towering steep,

...conceals, half discloses?

...of the morning's first beam

The Star-Spangled Banner

The Star-Spangled Banner

The Making of an American Icon

Lonn Taylor, Kathleen M. Kendrick, and Jeffrey L. Brodie

FOREWORD BY Ralph Lauren

PUBLISHED IN ASSOCIATION WITH

The National Museum of American History

Kenneth E. Behring Center

✸ Smithsonian Books

C Collins

An Imprint of HarperCollinsPublishers

The Star-Spangled Banner Preservation Project

is made possible by major support from

Polo Ralph Lauren

Significant leadership and support is provided by

The Pew Charitable Trusts
United States Congress
American Express
The John S. and James L. Knight Foundation

with special thanks to

First Lady Hillary Rodham Clinton
and the White House Millennium Council

and

Save America's Treasures at the National Trust for Historic Preservation

for their leadership

Cover: Composite photograph of the Star-Spangled Banner, 2004
Frontispiece: The Star-Spangled Banner, 1907
Endpapers: Manuscript of "The Star-Spangled Banner," written by Francis Scott Key, 1814 (courtesy Maryland Historical Society)

Edited by Amy Smith Bell
Proofread by Sharon Rose Vonasch
Indexed by Candace Hyatt
Designed by Jeff Wincapaw with assistance by Tina Kim
Color separations by iocolor, Seattle
Produced by Marquand Books, Inc., Seattle
  www.marquand.com
Printed in China by Toppan

FIRST EDITION

08 09 10 ID/TOP 10 9 8 7 6 5 4 3 2 1

Library of Congress Cataloging-in-Publication Data
Taylor, Lonn, 1940–
    The Star-Spangled Banner : the making of an American icon /
    by Lonn Taylor, Kathleen M. Kendrick, and Jeffrey L. Brodie ;
    foreword by Ralph Lauren.—1st ed.
        p. cm.
    Includes bibliographical references and index.
    ISBN 978-0-06-088562-5
    1. Baltimore, Battle of, Baltimore, Md., 1814. 2. United States—History—War of 1812—Flags. 3. Flags—United States—History. 4. National Museum of American History (U.S.). 5. Flags—Conservation and restoration—United States—Case studies. 6. Armistead, George, 1780–1818—Family. 7. Star-spangled banner (Song)—History. 8. Key, Francis Scott, 1779–1843. I. Kendrick, Kathleen M. II. Brodie, Jeffrey L. III. Title.
    E356.B2T395 2008
    929.9'20973—dc22   2007050482

CONTENTS

FOREWORD RALPH LAUREN

I love this country. I love being an American. My earliest memory of the Star-Spangled Banner was the flag that flew from the flagpole in the schoolyard across the street from my childhood home in the Bronx where we played baseball and basketball. Accompanying that memory was the incredible experience of rising to our feet at the start of a ball game in Yankee Stadium to sing our national anthem along with my hero, Joe DiMaggio, and all those thousands of fans. I remember pledging my allegiance to the flag each morning in school. It was a simpler time, after a world war, when those broad stripes and bright stars stood for our homeland and the freedom and hope it brought to every American.

I have always loved things that are worn, like an old plaid shirt that has been patched and mended or an old pickup truck that is a little dented and the paint a little faded. That patina is evidence of a history of work and a kind of honesty that to me is very American. It was in the late 1990s when I first heard about the Star-Spangled Banner Preservation Project. I was personally inspired to have Polo Ralph Lauren help save our greatest American treasure—the original Star-Spangled Banner. Understanding that this almost two-hundred-year-old hand-sewn piece of art was rapidly deteriorating but could be saved for future generations, we made a commitment. I particularly love that the preservation effort, applying cutting-edge scientific techniques and the knowledge of the best conservators, has not artificially changed the original flag. When you visit it in its new home at the Smithsonian's National Museum of American History, you experience some of the same emotion that inspired Francis Scott Key to pen "The Star-Spangled Banner." The ragged edges, patches, and holes are still there, and although its stripes are tattered and its stars are faded, it has endured—"our flag was," and is, "still there."

On September 11, 2001, three firefighters climbed on top of a mountain of the twisted remains of the World Trade Center to raise our flag. In the days and weeks that followed, images of the Stars and Stripes were seen everywhere—on the streets of New York, all across America, and all over the world. It was a symbol, like the Star-Spangled Banner flying over Fort McHenry, like the U.S. Marines hoisting the flag on Iwo Jima, that our flag and our nation and the memory of all those lost that day are still there.

I am a product of the American dream, and the flag is its symbol. Its preservation and conservation is imperative so that those who succeed us will understand our nation's heritage and the ideals on which the United States was founded. The Star-Spangled Banner was an inspiration to Francis Scott Key, it's been an inspiration for me, and now it will be an inspiration for future generations.

PREFACE

The Smithsonian Institution is the guardian of America's cultural heritage. For more than 150 years, the Smithsonian has collected and preserved objects that represent and document the nation's collective history. Perhaps no other object tells a more compelling story about the beginnings of our country than the Star-Spangled Banner, the flag that flew over Baltimore's Fort McHenry in 1814 and inspired Francis Scott Key to write the patriotic poem that later became the national anthem.

Today, over a century after the Smithsonian first acquired the Star-Spangled Banner, the National Museum of American History has constructed a new home for this cherished national icon. The unveiling of this monumental display chamber, located in the heart of the newly renovated Museum, marks the culmination of the Star-Spangled Banner Preservation Project, a major effort to conserve the nearly two-hundred-year-old flag. Beginning in the mid-1990s, the Museum has carried out a comprehensive plan to stabilize the fragile flag and create a unique gallery that would not only protect the Star-Spangled Banner but also illuminate its rich history and evoke its enduring significance as a national symbol. This innovative gallery is a testament to the skill and dedication of dozens, even hundreds of individuals—including architects, conservators, curators, educators, engineers, exhibition designers, and scientists, among many others—who have worked together to make the Star-Spangled Banner Preservation Project a triumphant success.

In carrying out the vital work of saving the Star-Spangled Banner, the National Museum of American History is truly grateful for the generous support of all our sponsors. The catalyst was First Lady Hillary Rodham Clinton's White House Millennium Council and its Save America's Treasures program, which provided invaluable leadership and marshaled both public and private resources. Support from the Pew Charitable Trusts, United States Congress, and the John S. and James L. Knight Foundation launched the planning and research, but what made the larger project a reality was an extraordinary gift from Polo Ralph Lauren through the Save America's Treasures program. Mr. Lauren's generosity extended beyond the preservation of the flag; it included his support for a national advertising campaign in association with Save America's Treasures at the National Trust for Historic Preservation. This campaign inspired many more donations from individuals and organizations across the country. Once the renovation work was under way, the Museum received additional generous grants for the project from American Express and the McCormick Tribune Foundation. The Smithsonian is grateful to all for their superb leadership in preserving the Star-Spangled Banner.

Although the National Museum of American History is the keeper of the flag, we are privileged to share the responsibility for preserving and interpreting the history of the

Star-Spangled Banner with several other institutions. The Fort McHenry National Monument and Historic Shrine, administered by the National Park Service, memorializes the defenders of Baltimore and the battle that gave birth to the national anthem. The original manuscript of "The Star-Spangled Banner," handwritten by Francis Scott Key in 1814, is in the collections of the Maryland Historical Society in Baltimore. At the Flag House and Star-Spangled Banner Museum, a National Historic Landmark, visitors can tour the house where Mary Pickersgill made the Fort McHenry flag and learn about life in Baltimore during the War of 1812. The dedicated staff and volunteers of these institutions have been valuable collaborators throughout the course of the Star-Spangled Banner Preservation Project, and we greatly appreciate all they have done and continue to do to help educate the public about the flag and its history. In helping to bring this message to an even wider audience, the Museum extends its thanks to the History Channel, a longtime partner and supporter of the project, for producing educational programs and materials about the Star-Spangled Banner that have reached millions nationwide.

The outpouring of support the Smithsonian has received for the Star-Spangled Banner Preservation Project reflects the special place that the flag occupies in the hearts of the American people. Though tattered and faded by time, the Star-Spangled Banner remains a resilient and powerful symbol of the American Dream—the ideals, values, and traditions that have defined our national experience. With the completion of this major undertaking and the opening of the redesigned Flag Hall, the National Museum of American History begins a new chapter in its ongoing mission to protect the Star-Spangled Banner and ensure that its "broad stripes and bright stars" will continue to inspire us all for generations to come.

Brent D. Glass
Director, National Museum of American History

Star Spangled Banner

SONG & CHORUS

AND THE STAR SPANGLED BANNER IN TRIUMPH SHALL WAVE,
O'er the land of the Free and the home of the Brave

2½

BUFFALO,
Published by BLODGETT & BRADFORD, 209 Main St.

ROCHESTER,
J. M. WILLSON.

CLEVELAND,
S. BRAINARD & CO.

NEW-YORK,
FIRTH, POND & CO.

THE STAR-SPANGLED BANNER— ARTIFACT AND ICON

This Star-Spangled Banner and all its successors have come to embody our country, what we think of as America. . . . You can neither honor the past, nor imagine the future, without the kind of citizenship embodied by all our memories of this flag.

—President William J. Clinton, July 13, 1998

On the morning of September 14, 1814, jubilant U.S. soldiers raised a huge American flag over Fort McHenry in Baltimore, Maryland, to signal a crucial victory over British forces during the War of 1812. Francis Scott Key, a lawyer and amateur poet who had witnessed the intense battle from a truce ship several miles downriver, glimpsed the broad stripes and bright stars waving over the fort. The sight inspired him to write a patriotic tribute to "that Star-Spangled Banner" and those who had defended it, creating a popular song that eventually became America's national anthem.

Today, when Americans hear "The Star-Spangled Banner," few think of Francis Scott Key or the War of 1812. Although such phrases as the "rockets' red glare" and "bombs bursting in air" refer to the events of a specific battle, the lyrics as a whole evoke universal feelings of patriotism, courage, and resilience. The song's reassuring message that "our flag was still there" has resonated throughout history in other times of national crisis—from the Civil War, to World War II, to the terrorist attacks of September 11, 2001. Its concluding refrain—"O say does that Star-Spangled Banner yet wave / O'er the land of the free and the home of the brave?"—is a question that every generation has continued to ask and struggled to affirm, in diverse and often contested ways.

"Star-Spangled Banner" song sheet, published by Blodgett & Bradford, New York, circa 1861.

By the time the United States Congress designated it as the official national anthem in 1931, "The Star-Spangled Banner" had outgrown the historical moment that inspired it and taken on a broader cultural significance. Likewise, the actual flag that Key saw that September morning in 1814, preserved today by the Smithsonian Institution's National Museum of American History, has come to represent something much greater to the nation than the victory of a single battle. It embodies not only the memories of Francis Scott Key and the defenders of Fort McHenry, but also the story of how one symbol came to define and inspire an entire nation.

The meanings and memories embodied by the Star-Spangled Banner, both the flag and the song, reflect the evolving role of the American flag in American life. From its practical origins during the Revolution as a tool for identifying U.S. ships and forts, the flag eventually became the primary emblem of American identity, ideals, and aspirations. This change did not happen overnight, however; rather, it was the result of an accumulation of meaningful encounters with the flag, dramatic moments that evoked strong patriotic feelings and embedded the Stars and Stripes in popular memory. Today we carry images of such moments from photographs and television—marines hoisting the flag on Iwo Jima, astronauts planting the flag on the moon, firefighters raising the flag at Ground Zero. In 1814, Americans experienced a similar kind of shared moment through the words of Francis Scott Key's poem, which was published and broadly circulated in the weeks after the Battle of Baltimore. By giving the flag a starring role in one of the most celebrated victories of the War of 1812, Key established a new prominence for the national emblem. And by naming it the Star-Spangled Banner, he transformed the flag into something familiar and personal that all Americans could claim as their own.

The Star-Spangled Banner, the garrison flag of Fort McHenry, was made in 1813 by Baltimore flagmaker Mary Pickersgill. Originally measuring thirty by forty-two feet, the giant banner had fifteen stars and fifteen stripes, the standard U.S. flag design from 1795 to 1818. Like all national flags made since 1777, when Congress established the original design of thirteen stars and stripes, the Star-Spangled Banner was first and foremost a utilitarian object. Its primary purpose was to identify an American military installation. Contrary to popular myths that emerged decades later, the national flag did not play a significant cultural role during the Revolution; instead, other symbols like the eagle, Lady Liberty, or George Washington were more popular expressions then of national identity and ideals.

That would start to change, however, during the War of 1812. Although largely forgotten today, the conflict some called the "Second War of Independence" represented a critical moment for the young nation. In declaring war on Great Britain, the United States sought to prove itself in the international arena as a sovereign power to be reckoned with. Fueled by expansionist visions of Republican congressmen known as the War Hawks, it was also one of the most controversial wars in American history, provoking sharp debate and division along political, economic, and regional lines. Among those who opposed the war was Francis Scott

Ambrotype portrait of a woman believed to be a freed slave who worked as a laundress for the Union army in Richmond, Virginia, during the Civil War.

Key, who wrote to a friend in 1813 that he would rather see the American flag lowered in disgrace than see it signaling victory in a war he considered immoral and unjust.[1]

By the time British forces launched their attack on Fort McHenry, however, Key's perspective had changed a great deal. Just weeks before, on August 24, 1814, he had witnessed the British invasion and burning of Washington, D.C., following the overwhelming defeat of American troops at Bladensburg, Maryland. When he was later dispatched to Baltimore to negotiate the release of an American prisoner, Key found himself once more an eyewitness to history, detained on a ship during the British bombardment. The exultant song he wrote on the morning of September 14 not only celebrated a military victory but captured a moment of personal revelation and connection to the national symbol. Through his written tribute to that Star-Spangled Banner, Key shared a patriotic vision that would shape how many other Americans looked at their flag for generations to come.

In the decades that followed the War of 1812, the American flag became an increasingly popular feature of political and cultural life, used by a multitude of groups—from abolitionists to nativists—to express their attachment to various ideas and causes. Yet during that time the original Star-Spangled Banner—the flag that had waved over Fort McHenry and inspired Key—was largely unknown outside of Baltimore. Guarded as a precious family relic by the descendants of Lieutenant Colonel George Armistead, who commanded the fort during the bombardment, the flag remained a treasure of local history, closely tied to the events of September 1814 and the memories of those who defended Baltimore. The Armisteads occasionally allowed the flag to be displayed for patriotic ceremonies, including the visit of General Marquis de Lafayette to Fort McHenry in 1824. In keeping with a common practice

Goddess of Liberty weathervane, manufactured by Cushing & White, Waltham, Massachusetts, circa 1870.

Patriotic pageant staged by Jewish immigrants in Milwaukee, Wisconsin, 1919.

of the time, they also cut pieces from the famous banner to present to veterans and other honored citizens. But during the Civil War, while "The Star-Spangled Banner" served as a favorite battle hymn for the Union, the flag itself was hidden away by the Armistead family—which included Confederate sympathizers—and remained unseen and unknown by the American public.

In 1873 naval officer and flag historian George Preble rediscovered the Star-Spangled Banner, which was then in the custody of Georgiana Appleton, George Armistead's daughter. With Appleton's encouragement Preble brought the flag into the national spotlight, arranging for it to be photographed for the first time at the Boston Navy Yard and displaying it at the New England Historic Genealogical Society. Preble also distributed additional "snippings" from the flag as souvenirs for his antiquarian friends and published articles about its history.

The enthusiasm shown for the Star-Spangled Banner during this period reflected the growing appetite for national history and patriotic symbols that accompanied the U.S. Centennial of 1876, as well as a heightened sense of reverence for the flag that had emerged during the Civil War. To ensure that these sentiments would be preserved and passed down to future generations, veterans and heritage societies began promoting patriotic education for children and immigrants. New rules and rituals also encouraged respect and veneration for the American flag. The Pledge of Allegiance, written for a nationwide public-school celebration of Columbus Day in 1892, became a daily tradition in American classrooms. At the turn of the twentieth century the military practice of rising for "The Star-Spangled Banner" was adopted at civilian events, including concert performances and baseball games. A civilian code of flag etiquette, established in 1923, defined the proper ways to use and display the national emblem.

This growing interest in promoting a national culture encouraged support for institutions that would collect, preserve, and display important artifacts of American history. The Smithsonian Institution, founded as a scientific research organization in 1846, began to take a leading role in this effort during the last quarter of the nineteenth century. This expansion of the Smithsonian's mission was prompted by the 1876 Centennial Exhibition in Philadelphia, which provided the Institution with national visibility as well as new collections that required the construction of a new museum building on the National Mall. In the 1880s a collection of George Washington memorabilia long displayed at the U.S. Patent Office was transferred to the Smithsonian, forming the basis of a new division of "Historical Relics" that continued to grow and develop over the next century. By the early 1900s the Smithsonian had established itself as a truly national museum, housing great works of art and significant historical artifacts along with vast collections of scientific specimens.

At the same time the Star-Spangled Banner had advanced far beyond its value as a family relic to become an artifact of recognized national significance. After Eben Appleton, George Armistead's grandson, inherited the flag in 1878, he became overwhelmed with the responsibility of caring for the banner and responding to demands for its display. He began to seek a public home for the flag that would befit its historical importance. In 1907, Appleton agreed to loan the flag to the Smithsonian Institution, and in 1912 he made it a permanent gift to the nation. In acquiring the Star-Spangled Banner and promoting its value as a national treasure, the Smithsonian also defined and reinforced its own importance as a caretaker of the nation's heritage.

When the flag arrived at the Smithsonian in 1907, it was already in tattered and fragile condition. The years—and the souvenir hunters—had taken their toll on the flag, leaving the Star-Spangled Banner eight feet shorter, with one fewer star, and too weak to support its own weight. In 1914, the one hundredth anniversary of the battle at Fort McHenry, the Smithsonian hired professional flag restorer Amelia Fowler to stabilize the flag so that it could be safely displayed for the long term. Using Fowler's patented technique, a team of needlewomen stitched the flag to a linen backing, which enabled the flag to be hung inside a glass case in the Arts and Industries Building. The Star-Spangled Banner remained there for the next half century, except for a brief period during World War II, when it was taken out of Washington, D.C., for safekeeping in case of enemy attack.

In 1964 the Star-Spangled Banner became the symbolic centerpiece of a new Smithsonian museum on the National Mall. The Museum of History and Technology, later renamed the National Museum of American History, was created to provide a permanent home for the Star-Spangled Banner and other historical treasures—from Thomas Jefferson's desk and Abraham Lincoln's hat to First Ladies' gowns and Edison's lightbulb. Impressively displayed

Vietnam Veterans Against the War march in Washington, D.C., April 1971.

New York City firefighters raising the flag at Ground Zero, September 11, 2001.

in the Museum's Flag Hall, suspended on a vertical backdrop that camouflaged its missing sections, the Star-Spangled Banner was transformed from a tattered relic into a patriotic icon. For the next thirty-five years millions of visitors to the National Museum of American History would encounter and remember the Star-Spangled Banner in this monumental way.

Outside the Museum, however, the American flag bore little resemblance to the static icon inside Flag Hall. Whether planted on the moon, carried in marches, waved with pride, or burned in protest, the flag was a dynamic and contested part of American life during the last four decades of the twentieth century. It served as a potent symbol in debates over civil rights and the Vietnam War, with opposing sides both claiming the flag to identify their cause with American ideals and values. The flag itself became a political issue in clashes over flag-desecration laws, controversial renditions of the national anthem, and the recitation of the Pledge of Allegiance in public schools. Throughout these years of keenly felt cultural and social divisions, it often seemed the flag was more capable of pulling Americans apart than bringing them together.

Immigrants' rights rally,
Washington, D.C., 2006.

The tragic events of September 11, 2001, changed that perspective, perhaps if only for a brief moment. On that afternoon, following the terrorist attacks on the World Trade Center, three New York City firefighters stood amid the smoking rubble and raised an American flag. That scene, strikingly captured by newspaper photographer Thomas E. Franklin and reproduced countless times in the aftermath of the attacks, came to define the memory of that day for many Americans. In a time of crisis and uncertainty, the raising of the flag at Ground Zero conveyed a message of unity, resilience, and pride. It offered people something to hold onto, a reassuring reminder of shared ideals and values to carry them through the tragedy and turmoil of the present. Buildings and lives may have been destroyed, but the nation would endure, because the flag was still there.

By drawing inspiration from the flag after 9/11, Americans participated in a tradition that has been repeated and passed down from one generation to the next for nearly two centuries. Just as it had for Francis Scott Key and a young nation in September 1814, the flag took on new and powerful meanings for the American people in September 2001. Raised over the ruins and recovered from the rubble, flown from houses and car antennas, worn on T-shirts and lapels, the flag was suddenly everywhere—emerging to decorate the American landscape as it had done at the outbreak of the Civil War in 1861 and again following the attack on Pearl Harbor in 1941. Once again, Americans invested this familiar symbol with fresh significance, finding in its broad stripes and bright stars a welcome source of comfort and community, an enduring connection to the nation, to the past, and to one another.

As the nation was discovering new meaning in the American flag, the original Star-Spangled Banner was undergoing a major transformation of its own. In 1996 the National Museum of American History had begun a project to evaluate the condition of the historic flag, which had been on exhibit in Flag Hall for more than thirty years. Curators, historians, textile conservators, and other experts convened at the Museum to determine how best to study, treat, and stabilize the flag for future display. In the summer of 1998 the Star-Spangled Banner Preservation Project was formally launched as part of the Save America's Treasures program, a public-private venture of the White House Millennium Council and the National Trust for Historic Preservation. The flag was taken down and moved into a custom-built laboratory on the Museum's second floor, where conservators worked on the flag in full view of the public: removing the linen backing that was attached in 1914, cleaning the flag, and attaching it to a new, lightweight support backing.

This preservation effort, the largest undertaking of its kind, applied cutting-edge scientific techniques to the study and care of the historic flag and yielded new insights about its condition. Using this information, conservators and curators worked with architects, engineers, and exhibit designers to develop a new permanent display chamber for the Star-Spangled Banner, which became the centerpiece of a major architectural renovation of the National Museum of American History building. To protect the fragile, nearly two-hundred-year-old textile from further damage and deterioration, today's flag chamber features low light levels, a display angle of no greater than ten degrees of elevation, stable temperature and relative humidity levels, a "clean room" environment, and physical security systems. Along with ensuring the long-term preservation of this cherished artifact, the new Star-Spangled Banner exhibition presents the history of the flag and explores its significance as a national symbol.

Today, visitors who come to the National Museum of American History to see the Star-Spangled Banner encounter a very different flag than what was first displayed in 1964. Rather than the intact icon hanging high overhead, the flag is now presented on a table, at eye level. The ragged edges, patches, and holes are plainly visible. No effort has been made to restore the flag to its original condition, to conceal the damage or make it look "like new." By showing the Star-Spangled Banner in its true condition, the Museum encourages visitors to see the flag as an artifact as well as an icon—as a treasured piece of American history that evokes the presence of the past as well as a shared symbol that embodies diverse meanings and memories. Although its stripes are tattered and its stars faded, the flag endures: it is, indeed, still here. As it did for Francis Scott Key nearly two centuries ago, the Star-Spangled Banner continues to inspire Americans to reflect on the ideals that unite us, the experiences we share, and the heritage we hold in trust for future generations.

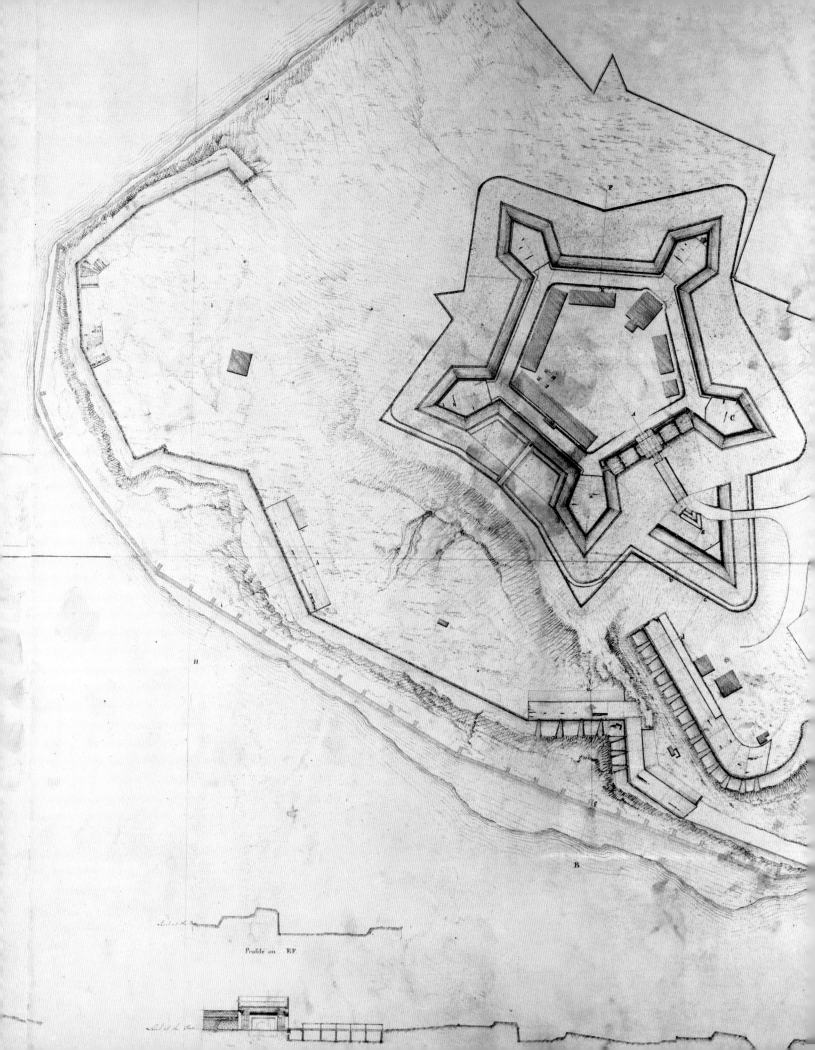

Profile on EF.

THE BATTLE OF BALTIMORE

Rejoice, ye people of America! Inhabitants of Philadelphia, New York, and Boston rejoice!
Baltimore has nobly fought your battles! Thank God, and thank the people of Baltimore!
—"A Republican paper of Boston," October 1, 1814

"Plan and Profiles of Fort
McHenry, 1819" (detail), by
Captain William Tell Poussin,
U.S. Topographical Engineers.
This drawing depicts the fort
as it likely appeared during the
British bombardment. Although
the fort's main structure is a
pentagon, the five bastions
projecting from the corners
inspired its common name,
the "star fort."

On August 1, 1814, a convoy of transports carrying five thousand British
troops commanded by Major General Robert Ross and a fleet of warships led
by Vice Admiral Sir Alexander Cochrane headed from the British naval station
in Bermuda toward the eastern coast of the United States. The British force
sought to wreak havoc on the upstart republic's capital at Washington, D.C.,
and on the city of Baltimore. With its handful of federal buildings and popula-
tion of fewer than ten thousand, Washington was mainly a symbolic target, an
opportunity to retaliate for American actions in British Canada and humiliate
the administration of President James Madison.

The capture of Baltimore, however, was a more ambitious and significant goal. The third-largest city in the United States, Baltimore also served
as home base for privateers, armed private vessels operating under government license, which had captured or sunk five hundred British merchant
ships in the two years since the War of 1812 had begun. British resentment
against the thriving American port ran high; the London press had clam-
ored for the destruction of the city, calling it a "nest of pirates." Moreover,
with peace negotiations between England and the United States at a standstill, a successful attack on Baltimore would not only exact revenge on the

Action between the USS
Constitution and the HMS
Guerriere, August 19, 1812.
Painting by Michel Felice
Corne. This battle, the first
major victory for the U.S.
Navy during the War of 1812,
earned the frigate *Constitution*
its famous nickname, "Old
Ironsides."

Ship model of the privateer *Lynx*. Built in 1812 by Thomas Kemp in Fells Point, Maryland, this topsail schooner was one of the fast and famous ships known as the Baltimore Clippers. Soon after it was launched as a blockade runner, *Lynx* was captured by the British.

privateers but also give England potential leverage to force an end to "Mr. Madison's War" on British terms.[1]

A turning point in the history of the young republic, the War of 1812 began because Great Britain, engaged in a life-or-death struggle with Napoleon's France, had tried to prevent American ships from trading with France. British ships hovered outside of American seaports, stopping American ships, confiscating their cargoes, and impressing American sailors among their crews into British service. Incensed by this interference, the U.S. Congress declared war on June 18, 1812. Western congressmen known as the War Hawks saw the war as an opportunity to seek annexation of British Canada. As soon as war was declared, an American army invaded Canada, but the British quickly repulsed their attack and occupied Detroit. British and U.S. military and naval forces clashed along the U.S.-Canadian border, on the Great Lakes, and in actions at sea, but they fought no decisive battles. Meanwhile, the British continued to devote most of their resources to defeating Napoleon in Europe.

Napoleon's abdication in April 1814 freed the British to intensify military actions against the United States. British reinforcements arrived in Canada with the intention of invading New York by way of Lake Champlain. A second convoy of ships and soldiers went to Bermuda, intending to conduct a series of raids in the Chesapeake Bay region and eventually to seize New Orleans.

President Madison's War Message to Congress

On June 1, 1812, President James Madison made the case for war against Great Britain in a confidential letter to Congress. Emphasizing British violations of American maritime rights, Madison argued that such acts not only insulted the United States but jeopardized American independence. Sixteen days later, Congress declared war on Great Britain. Although it was a victory for Madison and the War Hawks, the vote was close—only 61 percent in favor—the lowest support for a declaration of war in American history.[1]

To the Senate and House of Representatives of the United States:

I communicate to Congress certain documents, being a continuation of those heretofore laid before them, on the subject of our affairs with Great Britain.

Without going back beyond the renewal, in one thousand eight hundred and three, of the war in which Great Britain is engaged, and omitting unrepaired wrongs of inferior magnitude, the conduct of her Government presents a series of acts, hostile to the United States as an independent and neutral nation.

British cruisers have been in the continued practice of violating the American flag on the great high-way of nations, and of seizing and carrying off persons sailing under it; not in the exercise of a belligerent right, founded on the law of nations against an enemy, but a municipal prerogative over British subjects. . . . The practice, hence, is so far from affecting British subjects alone, that, under the pretext of searching for these, thousands of American citizens, under the safeguard of public law, and of their national flag, have been torn from their country, and from everything dear to them; have been dragged on board ships of war of a foreign nation, and exposed, under the severities of their discipline, to be exiled to the most distant and deadly climes, to risk their lives in the battles of their oppressors, and to be the melancholy instruments of taking away those of their own brethren. . . .

British cruisers have been in the practice also of violating the rights and the peace of our coasts. They hover over and harass our entering and departing commerce. . . . Under pretended blockades, without the presence of an adequate force, and sometimes without the practicability of applying one, our commerce has been plundered in every sea; the great staples of our country have been cut off from their legitimate markets; and a destructive blow aimed at our agricultural and maritime interests. . . .

We behold, in fine, on the side of Great Britain, a state of war against the United States; and on the side of the United States, a state of peace towards Great Britain. Whether the United States shall continue passive under these progressive usurpations, and these accumulating wrongs, or, opposing force to force in defence of their national rights, shall commit a just cause into the hands of the Almighty Disposer of events, avoiding all connexions which might entangle it in the contest or views of other Powers, and preserving a constant readiness to concur in an honorable re-establishment of peace and friendship, is a solemn question, which the Constitution wisely confides to the Legislative Department of the Government. In recommending it to their early deliberations, I am happy in the assurance that the decision will be worthy the enlightened and patriotic councils of a virtuous, a free, and a powerful nation.[2]

James Madison, president of the
United States during the War of 1812.
Portrait by John Vanderlyn, 1816.

This commemorative earthenware pitcher, made in Staffordshire, England, around 1815 for the American market, is inscribed with the rallying cry of the War of 1812: "Free Trade and Sailors' Rights."

Military drum made by Abner Stevens of Pittsfield, Massachusetts, 1812. The "Liberty or Death" banner clutched in the eagle's beak evokes the popular American view of the War of 1812 as the Second War of Independence.

Guided by Rear Admiral George Cockburn, whose ships had been blockading Chesapeake Bay and raiding the small towns on its shores all summer, the British fleet entered the bay on August 16, 1814, and made its way up the Patuxent River. While Major General Ross's troops landed at the town of Benedict, Maryland, Admiral Cockburn's boats pursued a flotilla of American gunboats under Commodore Joshua Barney up the river to Pig Point. There, Barney scuttled the gunboats. General Ross's troops marched across the neck of land separating the Patuxent and Potomac rivers toward Washington. On August 24, at Bladensburg, Maryland, General Ross's troops met and resoundingly defeated a hastily assembled American force twice their size under General William Henry Winder. The Americans broke and ran in the face of the disciplined ranks of British bayonets.

That night the British, led by General Ross and Admiral Cockburn, occupied Washington, where they methodically set fire to the U.S. Capitol, the president's mansion, and other public buildings. Many residents, including First Lady Dolley Madison, had already fled the city, taking with them such national treasures as the Declaration of Independence and Gilbert Stuart's portrait of George Washington to prevent their destruction by the enemy. Meanwhile, those who stayed behind watched helplessly as the young capital city went up in flames. "You never saw a drawing room so brilliantly lighted as the whole city was that night," wrote Washington resident Mary Stockton Hunter to her sister. "Few thought of going to bed—they spent the night in gazing on the fires and lamenting the disgrace of the city."[2] That disgrace was compounded a few days later when a British naval squadron commanded by Captain James Alexander Gordon appeared in the Potomac off Alexandria, Virginia. Responding to the pleas of merchants with warehouses full of tobacco and flour, Mayor Charles Simms surrendered.

The surrender backfired, however: the British confiscated the valuable goods and loaded them onto their ships.

By September 8, Ross, Cockburn, and their respective troops rejoined Admiral Cochrane and the rest of the British fleet at Tangier Island in Chesapeake Bay. The three commanding officers planned their strategy for capturing Baltimore. The plan called for a combined land and sea operation, beginning with a landing by Ross's troops at North Point, Maryland, at the mouth of the Patapsco River. Ross's troops were to march thirteen miles northwestward up Long Log Lane and the Philadelphia Road to the city of Baltimore. Meanwhile, Cochrane's ships would bombard Fort McHenry in order to enter Baltimore's inner harbor and support Ross's troops as they pressed their attack on the city.

In the days after the British burning of Washington, D.C., the people of Baltimore prepared themselves to meet the enemy. Although some responded to the news from Washington

"Capture of the City of Washington." Based on an engraving from *Rapin's History of England*, published by J. & J. Gundee, Albion Press, London, 1815.

Dolley Madison's Letter from Washington

In this famous letter First Lady Dolley Madison described her final anxious hours in the White House as British forces advanced on the nation's capital in August 1814. The letter, written to the First Lady's sister, Anna Cutts, first appeared publicly in the book *The National Portrait Gallery of Distinguished Americans*, published in Philadelphia in 1837. No original copy of the letter has been found; some historians have speculated that Madison may have composed the letter some years after the fact, based on her memories of past events. Regardless of when they were actually written, her words provide a suspenseful, lively account of the capture of Washington through the eyes of one of its most well-known and beloved residents.[1]

Tuesday Augt. 23d. 1814.

Dear Sister

My husband left me yesterday morng. to join Gen. Winder. He enquired anxiously whether I had courage, or firmness to remain in the President's house until his return, on the morrow, or succeeding day, and on my assurance that I had no fear but for him and the success of our army, he left me, beseeching me to take care of myself, and of the cabinet papers, public and private. I have since recd. two despatches from him, written with a pencil; the last is alarming, because he desires I should be ready at a moment's warning to enter my carriage and leave the city; that the enemy seemed stronger than had been reported, and that it might happen that they would reach the city, with intention to destroy it. . . . I am accordingly ready; I have pressed as many cabinet papers into trunks as to fill one carriage; our private property must be sacrificed, as it is impossible to procure wagons for its transportation. I am determined not to go myself until I see Mr. Madison safe, and he can accompany me, as I hear of much hostility towards him, . . . disaffection stalks around us. . . . My friends and acquaintances are all gone; Even Col. C with his hundred men, who were stationed as a guard in the enclosure. . . . French John (a faithful domestic) with his usual activity and resolution, offers to spike the cannon at the gate, and to lay a train of powder which would blow up the British, should they enter the house. To the last proposition I positively object, without being able, however, to

make him understand why all advantages in war may not be taken.

Wednesday morng., twelve o'clock. Since sunrise I have been turning my spyglass in every direction and watching with unwearied anxiety, hoping to discern the approach of my dear husband and his friends, but, alas, I can descry only groups of military wandering in all directions, as if there was a lack of arms, or of spirit to fight for their own firesides!

Three O'clock. Will you believe it, my Sister? We have had a battle or skirmish near Bladensburg, and I am still here within sound of the cannon! Mr. Madison comes not; may God protect him! Two messengers covered with dust, come to bid me fly; but I wait for him. . . . At this late hour a wagon has been procured, I have had it filled with the plate and most valuable portable articles belonging to the house; whether it will reach its destination; the Bank of Maryland, or fall into the hands of British soldiery, events must determine.

Our kind friend, Mr. Carroll, has come to hasten my departure, and is in a very bad humor with me because I insist on waiting until the large picture of Gen. Washington is secured, and it requires to be unscrewed from the wall. This process was found too tedious for these perilous moments; I have ordered the frame to be broken, and the canvass taken out it is done, and the precious portrait placed in the hands of two gentlemen of New York, for safe keeping. And now, dear sister, I must leave this house, or the retreating army will make me a prisoner in it, by filling up the road I am directed to take. When I shall again write you, or where I shall be tomorrow, I cannot tell!![2]

Dolley Madison, America's First
Lady during the War of 1812.
Portrait by Gilbert Stuart, 1804.

Ruins of the U.S. Capitol after burning by the British. Drawing by George Munger, circa 1814.

Charred timber from the White House fire of 1814. This relic of the burning of Washington was discovered 135 years later, when the White House underwent renovations during the Truman administration.

with despair and panic, many also vowed to stand their ground and fight. "Every American heart is bursting with shame and indignation at the catastrophe," admitted George Douglass, a Baltimore newspaper editor and militiaman. But those emotions had forged a new sense of unity and resolve to defend the city: "All hearts and hands have cordially united in the common cause. Everyday, almost every hour, bodies of troops are marching in to our assistance."[3]

Indeed, the attack on Washington had sparked a wave of patriotic feeling across the nation, as Americans from Virginia to New York imagined their homes could be the next target. "The questions are not now whether the war was just or unjust in its commencement," declared Mayor DeWitt Clinton of New York, a dissident Republican who had opposed the war and run against James Madison in the 1812 presidential election. "The present inquiry is: Will we defend our country, our city, our property, and our families? Will we go forth to meet and repel the enemy?" On September 1, President Madison issued a proclamation that condemned British "barbarism" and authorized local districts to call up their militia for defense against possible invasion. "On an occasion that appeals so forcibly to the proud feelings and patriotic devotion of the American people," he concluded, "none will forget what they owe to themselves, what they owe to their country and the high destinies which await it."[4]

Back in Baltimore, where the next battle lines were being drawn, the stakes were clear to Commodore John Rodgers, who had brought in naval forces from Philadelphia to help defend the port city. If the British attack was successful, he wrote to Secretary of the Navy William Jones on August 29, the path would be cleared for an invasion of Philadelphia—consequences Rodgers found "dreadful to ruminate on." Yet Rodgers was cheered by the "patriotic spirit" he witnessed among the citizens of Baltimore, noting their pledge "to defend the place to the last extremity."[5]

Major General Samuel Smith, a veteran of the Revolution and a leading Baltimore merchant, was in command of the city's defenses. Since the spring of 1813, when the British fleet launched an initial series of raids along the Chesapeake Bay, Smith had been mobilizing men and money to prepare the city for a possible attack. By September 1814 he had heavily fortified the eastern approaches to Baltimore in anticipation of an attack from that direction. Nearly fifteen thousand militiamen and a hundred pieces of artillery lined a half mile of trenches and earthworks along both sides of the Philadelphia Road along the crest of Hampstead Hill. More troops served as a forward line thrown across the narrow peninsula closer to North Point.

Smith paid particular attention to protecting Fort McHenry, which was about eight miles up the Patapsco from North Point and which guarded Baltimore Harbor. A floating barrier

To honor their heroic defense of the city during the War of 1812, the Baltimore City Council in 1816 commissioned these portraits of Major General Samuel Smith (left) and Lieutenant Colonel George Armistead (right), by the artist Rembrandt Peale.

The Defense of Baltimore: Assembling of the Troops, September 12, 1814. Thomas Ruckle, a corporal in the Maryland Militia who fought in the Battle of Baltimore, later painted this scene of American soldiers gathered on Hampstead Hill to intercept the British advance from North Point.

made of chained-together ship masts blocked the mouth of the harbor. Just beyond, a row of sunken hulks served as further deterrent. The fort itself was armed with fifty-seven 18-, 24-, and 36-pound naval guns and artillery pieces with a range of one and a half miles. Both inside the fort and in the earthworks around it, a 250-man artillery garrison, supplemented by nearly 750 battle-ready infantry regulars, sailors, and militiamen, prepared for battle. Commanding the U.S. troops at Fort McHenry was Major George Armistead, a professional regular army soldier who in 1813 had distinguished himself at the capture of Fort George from the British on the Canadian frontier.

From the beginning, the British did not anticipate the Americans' strong defense. Early on the morning of September 12, Ross's troops landed at North Point. Just after noon they encountered the American forward line. In the ensuing battle, an American sharpshooter killed General Ross, who had been riding back from the front of his line to call up reinforcements. The Americans withstood British fire for nearly an hour before withdrawing toward their main line.

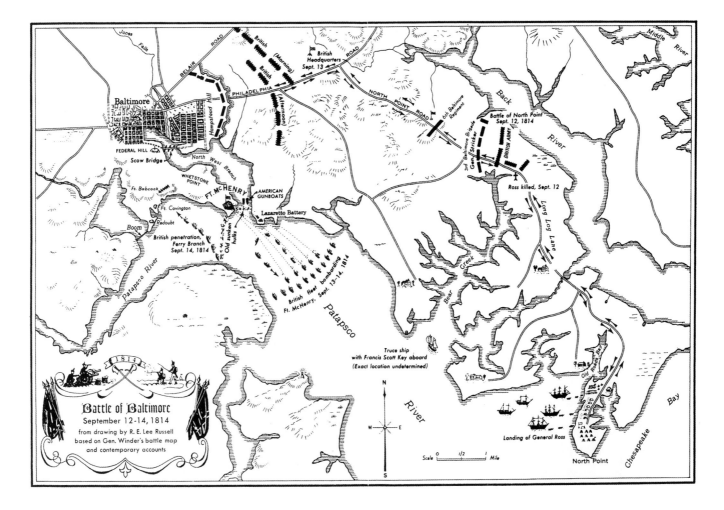

Map of the Battle of Baltimore, September 12–14, 1814.

The British spent a miserable, rainy night encamped on the battleground. Early the next morning, September 13, Lieutenant Colonel Arthur Brooke, who had assumed Ross's command, led his men forward to within sight of the American main line. Brooke immediately realized that he could not defeat the Americans in a daytime frontal attack. He spent the day maneuvering his troops in the rain and probing the American defenses for a possible night attack.[6]

THE BOMBARDMENT OF FORT McHENRY

By midafternoon on September 12 three British frigates—*Seahorse, Surprise,* and *Severn*—had anchored in the Patapsco about five miles from the fort. The bomb vessels *Meteor, Devastation, Aetna, Volcano,* and *Terror,* accompanied by the rocket ship *Erebus,* had approached to within two and a half miles, safely out of reach of the fort's guns. As the British maritime arsenal's most formidable weapons, the bomb vessels were specially constructed shallow-draft ships that carried ten- and thirteen-inch mortars with ranges of two miles. The mortars fired huge

[overleaf] "A View of the Bombardment of Fort McHenry." Print by J. Bower, Philadelphia, 1816.

Battle Monument erected by the City of Baltimore, begun in 1815 and completed in 1825. Photograph by John Plumbe, circa 1846.

Bombshell-shaped silver punchbowl, cups, ladle, and tray presented to Lieutenant Colonel George Armistead by the citizens of Baltimore, 1816.

spherical bombshells filled with powder that exploded over the target, scattering deadly shards of shrapnel. *Erebus* was armed with Congreve rockets, which carried large amounts of incendiary and explosive materials in their warheads. Fired in salvos, the rockets made a terrifying whooshing noise as they passed overhead and ignited fires wherever they landed.

The British started bombarding the fort at 6:30 a.m. on September 13 and continued throughout the day and the following night. At first the fort returned the fire, but the British ships remained out of range of the fort's guns. At 10:00 in the morning Major Armistead ordered his gunners to cease firing. For the next few hours Armistead's men crouched in trenches and behind walls while the bombs burst around them. "We were like pigeons tied by the legs to be shot at," recalled Judge Joseph H. Nicholson, a commanding officer of the Artillery Fencibles, in a letter to Secretary of War James Monroe.[7]

At about 3:00 that afternoon the British bomb ships moved in for the kill, sailing within range of the fort's guns. The American gunners responded with fire that so badly damaged *Erebus* that the ship had to be towed back out of range. Also hit, *Devastation* and *Volcano* retreated to their previous positions and maintained their bombardment from a safe distance. The bombs continued to fall at the rate of nearly one a minute for the rest of the afternoon and into the night. The men in the fort watched the explosions light up the sky like lightning flashes. Baltimoreans could clearly see the stream of sparks from the bombs' fuses arching through the air. The sounds of a torrential rain, which had worsened during the

day, mixed with peals of thunder, which in turn joined the cacophony caused by the mortars, bombs, and rockets.

During that night the British strategy began to unravel. At about midnight Admiral Cochrane decided that he had no chance of getting his ships past Fort McHenry and the line of sunken ships that blocked the entrance to the harbor. He sent Lieutenant Colonel Brooke a message to that effect. At about the same time an elite group of twelve hundred British marines and seamen led by Captain Charles Napier set out from Cochrane's ships to create a diversion that would aid Brooke's night attack even if the larger ships could not get into the harbor. Napier's men set out in the dark in a single file of barges with muffled oars, aiming to disembark behind Fort McHenry in the Ferry Branch of the Patapsco. In the darkness and rain, however, the last nine boats in the line got lost and headed instead toward the inner harbor. The other boats were discovered by the alert artillerymen at Battery Babcock and Fort Covington, two of the batteries outside the fort.

After a fierce artillery duel the British barges retreated to their mother ships. Brooke reluctantly gave up any idea of attack and began to withdraw his troops back to their landing place at North Point. At about 2:00 in the morning the bomb vessels resumed their fire, which had been suspended until Napier's boats were safely back. By 4:00 a.m. the British slowed the bombing, and by about 7:00 that morning they stopped firing. Within two hours the defenders of the fort saw the bomb vessels and frigates move down the river to join the main fleet at North Point, where Brooke's men were about to start their embarkation. Just over twenty-four hours after launching their first bomb, the British had given up their attempt. Baltimore was saved.

"As the last vessel spread her canvas to the wind," wrote British midshipman Robert Barrett, who had witnessed the bombardment from the frigate *Hebrus*, "the Americans hoisted a most superb and splendid ensign on their battery, and fired at the same time a gun of defiance." Private Isaac Munroe, of the Baltimore Fencibles, saw the same flag and recorded it in a letter he wrote to a friend in Boston on September 17. "At dawn on the 14th," he wrote, "our morning gun was fired, the flag hoisted, Yankee Doodle played, and we all appeared in full view of a formidable and mortified enemy, who calculated upon our surrender in 20 minutes after the commencement of the action." The flag that both men saw was the flag now known as the Star-Spangled Banner.[8]

GEORGE ARMISTEAD AND THE "OLD DEFENDERS" HONORED

By September 16, 1814, the last British ship had left the harbor; the sky over Fort McHenry was still, except for the sounds of victory echoing from the city. Celebrations erupted up and down the East Coast, and Baltimoreans rejoiced that the city had been spared Washington's fate. Major George Armistead and his men, along with Major General Samuel Smith and his soldiers on Hampstead Hill, became instant heroes. Armistead took pride in the fact that his losses amounted to only four men killed and twenty-four wounded.

According to his estimate, fifteen hundred to eighteen hundred bombs had been fired at the fort, four hundred of which had fallen within its walls.

Baltimoreans took particular pleasure that the victory came just weeks after the cowardly Washingtonians had run away, leaving the British to burn their city. In their eyes a group of local citizens had defeated the greatest army and navy in the world. The veterans of North Point and Fort McHenry became known as the Old Defenders, and they marched in parades in Baltimore on September 12 for the rest of their lives. Celebrations on that day, known as Defenders' Day, have endured as a Baltimore tradition.

Although George Armistead became a hero in Maryland, he started life as a Virginian, born on his mother's Baylor family plantation, Newmarket, in Caroline County, on April 10, 1780. He was related to patrician Virginia families on both sides, but he also had important Baltimore ties. On October 26, 1810, during a previous tour of duty at Fort McHenry, he had married Louisa Hughes, the daughter of Christopher Hughes, a wealthy Baltimore silversmith and brickyard owner. Louisa's brother, Christopher Hughes Jr., was married to Sophia Smith, the daughter of Major General Samuel Smith, who was not only a hero of the Revolution but also a wealthy Baltimore merchant and a longstanding member of Congress. George and Louisa Armistead had four children: Mary Armistead (Bradford), Margaret Armistead (Howell), Christopher Hughes Armistead, and Georgiana Armistead (Appleton).[9]

Within days of the battle President James Madison promoted Armistead to the rank of brevet lieutenant colonel, citing his "gallant conduct . . . during the late attack and bombardment." The following September, on the first anniversary of the battle at North Point, the City of Baltimore invited Armistead, along with Major General Smith and General John Stricker, who had commanded the forward line at North Point, to lay the cornerstone for the Battle Monument in downtown Baltimore. A memorial to those who died at North Point and Fort McHenry, the Battle Monument still stands in the heart of Baltimore, and it has served as the city's official emblem since 1827.[10]

In 1816 the Baltimore City Council commissioned Baltimore artist Rembrandt Peale to paint Armistead's portrait to hang in the City Council Chamber. A group of citizens presented Lieutenant Colonel Armistead with what the *Niles' Weekly Register* described as "a superb piece of plate, resembling a bomb-shell, to serve as a great bowl by lifting the cover, with appropriate supporters, descriptions, and devices."[11] The silver service consists of an oval tray, a silver bowl with a cover supported by four silver eagles on a round base, a ladle, and ten silver cups. The bowl was made by Philadelphia silversmiths Thomas Fletcher and Sidney Gardiner, and the ladle and cups are marked by Andrew E. Warner of Baltimore. A view of Fort McHenry is engraved on one side, and an inscription appears on the other, as follows: "Presented by a number of citizens of Baltimore to Lt. Col. George Armistead for his gallant and successful defense of Fort McHenry during the bombardment by a large British force on the 12th and 13th of September when upwards of 1500 shells were thrown; 400 of which fell within the area of the Fort and some of them of the diameter of this vase."[12]

Lieutenant Colonel Armistead continued to be honored after his untimely death on April 25, 1818, at the age of thirty-nine. The cause of his death is not known. His funeral procession, which featured a number of military bands stationed along the route, was the largest that Baltimoreans had ever seen. Guns fired at one-minute intervals by an artillery battery on Federal Hill punctuated the ceremonies.

In 1827 the City of Baltimore erected a monument to Armistead at the City Spring on Saratoga Street. A marble tablet flanked by two marble cannons and surmounted by a flaming bomb, the monument later fell into disrepair. In 1861 it was dismantled and its remnants placed in storage. In 1882 the marble cannons and the flaming bomb were incorporated into a second monument to Armistead on Eutaw Place. This structure was later moved to Federal Hill, where it stands today, overlooking the very harbor Armistead defended. In 1914, as part of Baltimore's Star-Spangled Banner Centennial celebration, a third monument to Armistead, a bronze statue by Edward Berge, was erected on the grounds of Fort McHenry.[13]

A VICTORY FOR THE NATION
The heroic events of September 1814 helped bring the War of 1812 to a close. The American victory at Baltimore was matched by another on the northern frontier, where the British abandoned their advance toward New York when a U.S. naval squadron gained control of Lake Champlain on September 11 and severed the British supply line. After failing to take

Gold-mounted flintlock pistols presented to Commodore Thomas MacDonough by the State of Connecticut, commemorating his naval victory at the Battle of Lake Champlain, September 11, 1814.

Lieutenant Colonel George Armistead's Account of the Bombardment of Fort McHenry

The day after his great victory in Baltimore, Major Armistead suffered a physical collapse and was temporarily relieved of command. On September 24 he resumed his post at Fort McHenry, newly promoted to the rank of lieutenant colonel, and submitted his official report of the battle to Secretary of War James Monroe.

Fort McHenry, September 24th, 1814

Sir,

A severe indisposition, the effect of great fatigue and exposure, has prevented me heretofore from presenting you with an account of the attack on this post. On the night of Saturday the 10th inst. the British fleet, consisting of ships of the line, heavy frigates, and bomb vessels, amounting in the whole to 30 sail, appeared at the mouth of the river Patapsco, with every indication of an attempt on the city of Baltimore. My own force consisted of one company of U.S. artillery, under Capt. [Frederick] Evans, and two companies of sea fencibles, under Capts. [M.S.] Bunbury and [William H.] Addison. Of these three companies, 35 men were unfortunately on the sick list, and unfit for duty. I had been furnished with two companies of volunteer artillery from the city of Baltimore, under Capt. [John] Berry [Washington Artillerists] and Lt. Commandant [Charles] Pennington [Baltimore Independent Artillerists]. To these I must add another very fine company of volunteer artillerists, under Judge [Joseph H.] Nicholson [Baltimore Fencibles], who had proffered their services to aid in the defence of this post whenever an attack might be apprehended; and also a detachment from Commodore [Joshua] Barney's flotilla, under Lieut. [Solomon]

Rodman. Brig. Gen. [William] Winder had also furnished me with about six hundred infantry, under the command of Lieut. Col. [William] Steuart and Major [Samuel] Lane, consisting of detachments from the 12th, 14th, 36th, and 38th Regts. of U.S. troops—the total amounting to about 1000 effective men.

On Monday morning very early, it was perceived that the enemy was landing troops on the east side of the Patapsco, distant about ten miles. During that day and the ensuing night, he had brought sixteen ships (including five bomb ships) within about two miles and a half of this Fort. I had arranged my force as follows—The regular artillerists under Captain Evans, and the volunteers under Capt. Nicholson, manned the bastions in the Star Fort. Captains Bunbury's, Addison's, Rodman's, Berry's and Lieut. Commandant Pennington's command were stationed on the lower works, and the infantry under Lieut. Col. Steuart and Major Lane, were on the outer ditch, to meet the enemy at his landing, should he attempt one.

On Tuesday morning about sunrise, the enemy commenced the attack from his five bomb vessels, at the distance of about two miles, when, finding that his shells reached us, he anchored, and kept up an incessant and well directed bombardment. We immediately opened our batteries, and kept a brisk fire from our guns and mortars, but unfortunately our shot and shells all fell considerably short of him. This was to me a most distressing circumstance; as it left us exposed to a constant and tremendous shower of shells, without the most remote possibility of our doing him the slightest injury. It affords me the highest gratification to state, that although we were left exposed, and thus inactive, not a man shrunk from the conflict.

About 2 o'clock p.m. one of the 24 pounders on the south west bastion, under the immediate command of

Capt. Nicholson, was dismounted by a shell, the explosion from which killed his second Lieut., and wounded several of his men; the bustle necessarily produced in removing the wounded and remounting the gun probably induced the enemy to suspect that we were in a state of confusion, as he brought three of the bomb ships to what I believed to be good striking distance. I immediately ordered a fire to be opened, which was obeyed with alacrity through the whole garrison, and in half an hour those intruders again sheltered themselves by withdrawing beyond our reach. We gave three cheers, and again ceased firing. The enemy continued throwing shells, with one or two slight inter-missions, till one o'clock in the morning of Wednesday, when it was discovered that he had availed himself of the darkness of the night and had thrown a considerable force above to our right; they had approached very near to Fort Covington, when they began to throw rockets; intended, I presume, to give them an opportunity of examining the shores—as I have since understood; they had detached 1250 picket men, with scaling ladders, for the purpose of storming this fort. We once more had an opportunity of opening our batteries, and kept up a continued blaze for nearly two hours, which had the effect again to drive them off.

In justice to Lieut. [Henry] Newcomb, of the United States Navy, who commanded at Fort Covington, with a detachment of sailors, and Lieut. [John A.] Webster, of the flotilla, who commanded the Six Gun Battery, near that Fort, I ought to state, that during this time, they kept up an animated, and I believe a very destructive fire, to which I am persuaded, we are much indebted in repuls-ing the enemy. One of his sunken barges has since been found with two dead men in it—others have been seen floating in the river. The only means we had of directing our guns, was by the blaze of their rockets and the flashes of their guns. Had they ventured to the same situation in the day time, not a man would have escaped.

The bombardment continued on part of the enemy until 7 o'clock on Wednesday morning, when it ceased; and about nine, their ships got under weigh and stood down the river. During the bombardment, which lasted 25 hours (with two slight intermissions) from the best calculation I can make, from fifteen to eighteen hundred shells were thrown by the enemy. A few of these fell short. A large proportion burst over us, throwing their fragments among us, and threatening destruction. Many passed over, and about four hundred fell within the works. Two of the public buildings are materially injured—the others but slightly. I am happy to inform you (wonderful as it may appear) that our loss amounts only to four men killed, and 24 wounded. The latter will all recover. Among the killed, I have to lament the loss of Lieutenant [Levi] Clagget and Sergeant [John] Clemm, both of Capt. Nicholson's vol-unteers, two men whose fate is to be deplored, not only for their personal bravery, but for their high standing, amiable demeanor, and spotless integrity in private life. Lieut. Russell, of the company under Lieut. Pennington, received, early in the attack, a severe contusion in the heel; notwithstanding which, he remained at his post dur-ing the whole bombardment.

Were I to name any individual who signalized them-selves, it would be doing injustice to others. Suffice it to say, that every officer and soldier under my command did their duty to my entire satisfaction.

I have the honor to remain, respectfully, your obedient servant,

G. Armistead, Lt. Col. U.S.A.[1]

Uniform coat worn by General Andrew Jackson at the Battle of New Orleans, January 8, 1815.

"Gl. Jackson at the Battle of New Orleans." Lithograph by Charles Severin, printed by Boell & Michelin, New York, around 1856.

Baltimore, the British forces in the Chesapeake sailed for the Gulf of Mexico, where, reinforced by additional troops, they attempted to take New Orleans. On January 8, 1815, General Andrew Jackson and his corps of volunteers defeated the would-be invaders. The Americans ended the war in a blaze of glory. In fact, British and American representatives had already signed a peace treaty in Ghent, Belgium, on December 24, 1814, but word of peace did not reach North America until February 1815.

Although the Ghent treaty addressed none of the issues that caused the war, and no exchanges of territory took place, the War of 1812 severed the United States' remaining ties with the nation's colonial past. Dramatic victories at Baltimore and New Orleans showed the world that a new, untested nation with a novel form of government could bring the most powerful monarchy in the world to a standstill. The war ended debates within the republic about the validity of the new form of government. The triumphs freed Americans from the shadow of the mother country and demonstrated that the United States was a nation in its own right. By turning American eyes away from Europe and toward American resources, the War of 1812 opened the way for Americans to consider the needs of the future and the best means of national development.

Perhaps most significant, the war instilled in Americans a new sense of national pride. At a time when many feared the young nation was already losing the sense of unity and common purpose that had been forged during the War of Independence, the War of 1812 represented a new hope for reinvigorating those patriotic bonds. Albert Gallatin, one of the U.S. peace commissioners who negotiated the Treaty of Ghent, expressed it this way: "The war has renewed and reinstated the national feelings and character which the Revolution had given, and which were daily lessening. The people have now more general objects of attachment, with which their pride and political opinions are connected. They are more American; they feel and act more as a nation; and I hope that the permanency of the Union is thereby better secured."[14] After the Battle of Baltimore this sense of pride and attachment to the nation would find powerful expression in a song written by Francis Scott Key—and in the symbol he named the Star-Spangled Banner.

Flag of the Second Continental Light Dragoons. As they fought for national independence on the battlefield, Continental soldiers attached their loyalties to regimental banners that evoked ideals of freedom, valor, and home. This squadron flag, from a cavalry unit commissioned under Colonel Elisha Sheldon in 1776, features a canton of thirteen "liberty stripes" and the Latin motto: "Her country calls and her sons respond in tones of thunder."

First U.S. Silver Dollar. In April 1792 the United States Congress passed the Coinage Act, which created the U.S. Mint and established the dollar as the official unit of U.S. currency. The bill initially proposed that coins would depict the head of the current president, but this idea was rejected by Republicans and President George Washington himself as too monarchical. Instead, the act required coins to have "an impression emblematic of liberty" on the front and the eagle on the reverse.

MEANINGS AND MEMORIES SYMBOLS

Contrary to popular belief, the American flag did not play a major role in the War of Independence. Most of the myths about the flag's importance during the Revolution—including the famous tale of Betsy Ross sewing the first flag for General George Washington—emerged much later, after the Stars and Stripes had already become the nation's most significant and cherished icon. At the time the flag was created, however, it did not attract much attention from the general public; rather, its primary function was to identify ships and forts.

Instead of the flag, which was generally reserved for official use, ordinary Americans in the Revolutionary era turned to a variety of other symbols to express their patriotism and

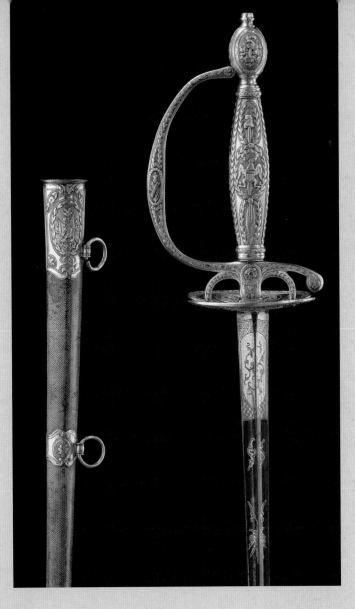

Presentation sword and scabbard. For leading a successful attack on British forces at Sag Harbor, Long Island, in May 1777, Lieutenant Colonel Return Jonathan Meigs received this elegant sword decorated with liberty caps, laurel wreaths, and the coat of arms of the United States. It is one of ten similar swords ordered by Congress to recognize Continental army officers for their service during the War of Independence.

Hong bowl. The United States' entry into the lucrative China trade in 1784 provided a vital opportunity for the new nation to assert its economic and political independence. On this Chinese export porcelain punch bowl, the American flag flies alongside the flags of Sweden, Great Britain, and other European countries on the waterfront in Canton, where Western merchants lived and conducted business in buildings known as "hongs."

OF A NEW NATION

define their national identity. Such figures as the eagle, Lady Liberty, and George Washington were more recognizable than the abstract stripes and stars, and they appeared as patriotic motifs on many objects of daily life during the early years of independence. Although the flag sometimes decorated these objects as well, it rarely stood on its own, because at the time it held few meaningful associations for most Americans.

That would start to change, however, during the War of 1812. Often referred to as the "Second War of Independence," the conflict inspired a fresh wave of patriotism in a generation too young to remember the Revolution. By giving the flag a starring role in one of the most celebrated victories of the war, Francis

Scott Key's song established a new prominence for the flag as an expression of national identity, unity, and pride. And by giving it a name—that Star-Spangled Banner—Key transformed the official emblem into something familiar and evocative, a symbol that Americans could connect with and claim as their own.

The artifacts on these pages reflect the diversity of national symbols that emerged during and after the American Revolution. Over time, as the flag accumulated more meanings and memories, it would gain a more prominent place in people's hearts and minds. But before it became the Star-Spangled Banner, the "new constellation" was only one symbol among many, its cultural significance yet to be determined.

BOTTOM LEFT
Fire bucket. Volunteer fire companies were an active and essential part of civic life during the early Republic. Firefighters often expressed their pride with elaborately decorated buckets such as this one, a rousing invocation to male heroism and patriotism. The portrait medallion of George Washington is framed by the legendary motto of Julius Caesar: "Veni, Vidi, Vici."

BOTTOM MIDDLE
Schoolgirl's picture. An example of how patriotic values were absorbed and expressed by young daughters of the Revolution, this delicate picture was made by an unknown pupil at Abby Wright's school for girls in South Hadley, Massachusetts, in 1809. Lady Liberty, clad in an empire-style dress, holds a flagpole topped with a liberty cap and an upturned cornucopia, a symbol of plenty.

BOTTOM RIGHT
Liverpool-type jug. After the Revolution, English manufacturers appealed to American consumers by exporting decorative ceramics that celebrated the new nation and honored its heroes. Entitled "Washington Crowned with Laurels by Liberty," this jug features a variety of early patriotic symbols, including the liberty cap, the eagle, and the American flag. A chain of fifteen links, each representing a state, frames the design.

Tavern sign. The proprietor of E. Stratton's Inn combined patriotic and practical symbols to draw customers into his New England establishment. One side of this wooden sign depicts an eagle with a shield clutching an olive branch and arrows in its talons, a pose adapted from the Great Seal of the United States, while the reverse has a wine decanter flanked by two goblets.

THE SONG

So long as patriotism dwells among us, so long will this song be the theme of our nation.

—*Baltimore American*, January 13, 1843

By the Dawn's Early Light. Color print after original painting by Edward Percy Moran, 1912–1913. This romanticized depiction of Francis Scott Key sighting the flag over Fort McHenry was created for the centennial anniversary of the Battle of Baltimore in 1914.

Of all the tributes paid to the American heroes of Fort McHenry, the most enduring is the victory song that became this country's national anthem. A thirty-five-year-old District of Columbia lawyer and amateur poet, Francis Scott Key was more than a bystander during the September 13–14 bombardment of Fort McHenry. He had accompanied John S. Skinner, a civilian employee of the Department of State, aboard one of the British ships to seek the release of an American civilian, Dr. William Beanes of Upper Marlboro, Maryland, who was being held prisoner. The British commanders Admiral Alexander Cochrane and General Robert Ross agreed to release Beanes, but they stipulated that all three Americans remain with the British fleet until the end of the attack on Baltimore.

Key and Skinner nervously paced the deck of their vessel all through the night, listening to the noise of the bombardment and straining to see through the smoke and rain if the American flag was still flying over Fort McHenry. While Key understood what was at stake in this battle, both for Baltimore and for the nation, his faith and his patriotism had been severely tested by recent events. A devout Episcopalian and a Federalist, he had opposed the War of 1812 on moral and political grounds. At one point he had even taken pleasure in his country's military failures, writing to a friend in 1813 that he would rather see the American flag lowered in disgrace than have it stand for persecution and dishonor, as he believed was the case in the United States' attempted invasion of British Canada.[1]

But when the enemy launched attacks along the Chesapeake Bay and threatened Washington, D.C., Key stepped forward to defend his native state and his home city. Just three weeks before the Battle of Baltimore, he had been at Bladensburg with the Georgetown militia, serving as aide to General Walter Smith. Key had witnessed the humiliating defeat of the American troops on August 24 and the subsequent burning of the nation's capital. Before leaving on his mission to rescue Beanes, Key had expressed feelings of doubt and despair in a letter to his father. "In these distressing times I really know not what I shall do to provide for the necessities of my family," he wrote, and concluded sadly, "There is no hope of peace."[2]

In light of all Key had experienced up to that moment, his relief at seeing the fort's garrison flag proudly flying over the battlements on the morning of September 14 takes on a deeper and more personal significance. Overcome with emotion, he started jotting down the beginnings of a poem on the back of a letter that was in his pocket, giving birth to the famous lines that would eventually become America's national anthem. In a speech delivered at a banquet in Frederick, Maryland, twenty years after the battle, Key recalled his feelings on that historic morning: "Through the clouds of war, the stars of that banner still shone . . . and I saw the discomfited host of its assailants driven back in ignominy to their ships. Then, in that hour of deliverance and joyful triumph, my heart spoke; and 'Does not such a country, and such defenders of their country, deserve a song?' was its question. With it came an inspiration not to be resisted; and even though it had been a hanging matter to make a song, I must have written it."[3]

When Francis Scott Key died on January 11, 1843, flags in both Washington and Baltimore were lowered to half-mast, and the U.S. Supreme Court adjourned for one day in his memory. Yet although Key's role as a witness to the dramatic battle was immortalized by his song, the poet himself never wrote a detailed account of the circumstances that surrounded his writing of the anthem. After Key's death, U.S. government agent John S. Skinner and Supreme Court Chief Justice Roger B. Taney, who was also Key's brother-in-law, each published accounts of those events. Skinner published an account in the *Baltimore Patriot and Gazette* on May 19, 1849. Taney wrote a letter to Charles Howard, Key's son-in-law, on March 17, 1856, that described at length a conversation he had with Key several weeks after the bombardment. In 1857, Robert Carter and Brothers published Taney's letter as an introduction to Henry V. D. Jones's *Poems of the Late Francis S. Key, Esq.* From these narratives historians have pieced together the story of how Key came to write "The Star-Spangled Banner."[4]

FRANCIS SCOTT KEY: EYEWITNESS TO HISTORY

Francis Scott Key's mission to the British fleet stemmed from an incident that occurred in the aftermath of the British burning of Washington, D.C. While the British retraced their steps to their landing place at Benedict, Maryland, and reembarked on their transports, a hundred or so stragglers remained behind, robbing farms along the roads between Washington and Benedict. On August 27, Dr. William Beanes, a leading citizen of Upper Marlboro whose house had served as Major General Ross's headquarters for a night during the British army's march toward Washington, organized a posse to stop the pillagers. Beanes and his companions rounded up several of the British marauders and locked them in the local jail. One of the soldiers escaped, however, and the next day a group of British cavalrymen arrested Beanes and his companions and took them to the British fleet as hostages.

When the Americans released their prisoners, the British freed all of their hostages except for Beanes. Major General Ross locked Beanes in the brig of Admiral Cochrane's flagship *Tonnant.* Beanes's friends and neighbors immediately set out to obtain his release. One such friend, Richard West, traveled to Georgetown to see Key, who was his wife's

The earliest known manuscript of "The Star-Spangled Banner," probably written on September 15, 1814, in Francis Scott Key's hand. Key is believed to have given this manuscript to his wife's brother-in-law, Judge Joseph H. Nicholson, who encouraged Key to publish his poem.

Francis Scott Key, author of "The Star-Spangled Banner." Portrait by Joseph Wood, circa 1825.

brother-in-law, and asked Key to negotiate for Beanes's freedom. On September 1, Key agreed to do what he could and went to see President James Madison, who referred him to General John Mason, the U.S. commissary general for prisoners.

On September 2, General Mason approved Key's mission and gave him a letter addressed to Ross, setting forth the government's case for Beanes's release as a civilian noncombatant. Mason instructed Key to go to Baltimore and contact Skinner, the U.S. government's agent for dealing with the British forces in the Chesapeake—Skinner would take Key to the British fleet. He had been the main means of communication between the government and the British blockading fleet in the Chesapeake for more than a year, and he was well known to Admiral Cockburn and his officers.

Key left for Baltimore on September 3, carrying with him Mason's letter to Ross as well as a bundle of letters from British soldiers who were prisoners in Washington. Some of the letters praised the Americans for giving medical assistance to wounded British troops. Key arrived in Baltimore on September 4, and the next day he and Skinner set out in a sixty-foot, flag-of-truce sloop, probably the *President*.[5] Skinner and Key found the British fleet down the Chesapeake, near the mouth of the Potomac, and were welcomed aboard the flagship *Tonnant*. That night they dined with General Ross and Admiral Cochrane and discussed Beanes's status. At some point in the evening, Ross was persuaded to release his prisoner. Taney's and Skinner's accounts agree that Key, Skinner, and Beanes were then told that, as witnesses to the preparations for the attack, including conversations between Ross and Cochrane, they would have to remain with the British fleet until after the attack on Baltimore. Cochrane arranged the men's transfer to the frigate *Surprise,* which then took their sloop in tow.

On Saturday, September 10, Cochrane agreed to return the Americans to their own sloop, along with a guard of British marines. On Sunday the fleet arrived at the mouth of the Patapsco River, and the flag-of-truce sloop was anchored somewhere in Old Roads Bay, northwest of North Point. It was from this vantage point that Key, Skinner, and Beanes heard the battle at North Point on September 12 and watched the bombardment on September 13 and 14. According to Taney, Key started composing his famous poem as he watched the enemy's bomb vessels pulling back toward the fleet and observed the flag streaming over the fort and did not finish the poem until minutes before reaching shore on September 16. Taney indicated that Key began with "brief notes . . . upon the back of a letter which he happened to have in his pocket."[6]

Key copied the four verses of the poem and on September 17 showed a copy to his wife's brother-in-law, Judge Joseph H. Nicholson, chief justice of the Baltimore courts, asking Nicholson what he thought of it. Judge Nicholson, who had commanded a volunteer company in the fort during the bombardment, reacted enthusiastically. Either he or Skinner—the accounts differ—took the poem to the office of the *Baltimore American,* where it was set in type and printed as a broadside. Entitled "Defence of Fort McHenry," the broadside featured a short introductory paragraph, likely written by Judge Nicholson, that described

the circumstances under which the lyrics were composed. It also contained the instruction that the words be sung to the tune "Anacreon in Heaven." The broadsides were taken to Fort McHenry, where every man received a copy. Judge Nicholson evidently kept one of Key's manuscript copies. That manuscript, which was passed on to Nicholson's granddaughter Rebecca Lloyd Shippen, is today in the collection of the Maryland Historical Society.

On September 20 the text was published in the *Baltimore Patriot,* and on September 21 in the *Baltimore American.* By mid-October 1814 it had been printed in at least seventeen other papers in cities along the East Coast. Sometime before November 18, Thomas Carr's music store in Baltimore published "The Star-Spangled Banner" in sheet-music form.

The first sheet-music issue of "The Star-Spangled Banner," printed by Thomas Carr's music store, Baltimore, 1814.

The Greek poet Anacreon, patron spirit of the Anacreontic Society. Sculpture by Eugène Guillaume, 1851, in the Musée d'Orsay, Paris.

NEW WORDS FOR AN OLD TUNE

"Anacreon in Heaven," the popular British tune Key chose to accompany his inspirational lyrics, was widely known in America during the early nineteenth century. Historians believe that Key probably had the melody in mind as he was composing the poem. At least a half-dozen American songbooks published before 1814, among them the two-volume *Baltimore Musical Miscellany* (1804 and 1805), included the tune. In 1805, Key himself had used the melody for a poem he wrote in honor of Captain Stephen Decatur, American naval hero and victor over the Barbary pirates, entitled "When the Warrior Returns from the Battle Afar."[7] That song, like "The Star-Spangled Banner," has four verses. It begins:

> *When the warrior returns from the battle afar*
> *To the home and the country he has nobly defended*
> *Oh, warm be the welcome to gladden his ear*
> *And loud be the joys that his perils are ended!*
> *In the full tide of our song, let his fame roll along*
> *To the feast flowing board let us gratefully throng*
> *Where mixed with the olive the laurel shall wave*
> *And form a bright wreath for the brow of the brave.*

The last two lines appear in each of the four verses. The third verse contains the couplet "And pale beamed the Crescent, its splendor obscured / By the star-spangled flag of our nation." The poem appears in Henry V. D. Jones's 1857 edition of Key's poems, just after "The Star-Spangled Banner."

"Anacreon in Heaven" is often misleadingly described as an old English drinking song. Its foreign, seemingly disreputable origin was advanced in the 1920s as an argument against congressional recognition of "The Star-Spangled Banner" as a national anthem. "Drinking song," in the sense of students with linked arms and raised steins, is in fact a misnomer. Actually the tune was written in 1775 or 1776 by John Stafford Smith, a London composer of secular and sacred music, to accompany words written by Ralph Tomlinson. It was the "constitutional song" of a mid- to late-eighteenth-century gentlemen's musical club called the Anacreontic Society, named for the sixth-century B.C.E. Greek poet Anacreon, who wrote a number of short verses in praise of wine and women.

About a dozen times a year Anacreontic Society members assembled in rooms above various London taverns to play instrumental music and dine together. Guests at the concerts included composers Franz Joseph Haydn and Johann Nepomuk Hummel, and the meetings were described in 1787 as being "conducted under the strictest influence of propriety and decorum." After a concert lasting two or so hours, the members would adjoin for a cold supper, followed by lighthearted songs performed by the members. The meeting continued with the singing of "Anacreon in Heaven," usually performed as a solo by the club's president. The words of the song invoked the spirit of the Greek poet to inspire the club's members:

To Anacreon in Heaven, where he sat in full glee,
A few sons of harmony sent a petition
That he their inspirer and patron would be;
When this answer arrived from the jolly old Grecian.
"Voice fiddle and flute, no longer be mute,
I'll lend you my name, and inspire you to boot,
And besides I'll instruct you like me to entwine
The myrtle of Venus with Bacchus's vine."

The song continued in the inspirational vein for three more verses.

No one has seriously doubted that Ralph Tomlinson penned the words, but late-nineteenth- and early-twentieth-century scholars debated who wrote the tune. Some advanced the names of Samuel Arnold, the last president of the Anacreontic Society, whereas others credited Turlough O'Carolan, an Irish composer who died in 1738. Still others contended that the song had its origins in an Irish tune called "Royal Inniskilling." In his 1909 *Report on "The Star-Spangled Banner,"* musicologist Oscar Sonneck was able to prove John Stafford Smith's authorship to most scholars' satisfaction. "The Star-Spangled Banner" is catalogued under the name of John Stafford Smith in libraries to this day.[8]

FROM POPULAR SONG TO NATIONAL ANTHEM

Although "The Star-Spangled Banner" did not earn its official status from the United States Congress until 1931, throughout the nineteenth century it was frequently referred to as a "national anthem." The belief that the United States should have only one anthem did not take hold until the 1890s. For decades after its publication in 1814, Key's song was one of many national airs—like "Hail Columbia" or "Yankee Doodle"—that Americans turned to for inspiration and entertainment. It was notably more popular in the Baltimore and Washington, D.C., region due to its connection with local events, but a thriving music-publishing industry, patriotic holiday celebrations, and the popular theater circuit helped bring the song to a national audience as well.

At a Baltimore theater on October 19, 1814, a Mr. Hardinge gave the first documented performance of "The Star-Spangled Banner." The performance, presented at the end of a play, evidently met with success, for it was repeated on November 12. By then, Thomas Carr was selling the first sheet-music edition of the song from his store in Baltimore, and numerous American newspapers, from Boston to Savannah, had reprinted the lyrics along with the story of how they were composed. The anthem also appeared in four songsters published that year in three different states: *American Patriotic and Comic Modern Songs,* from Newburyport, Massachusetts; *The American Muse* and *The Columbian Harmonist,* both from New York; and *The National Songster,* from Hagerstown, Maryland. Music publishers across the country continued to issue new editions of the song over the next fifty years, with a significantly increased number emerging around the time of the Civil War.[9]

Although Americans could buy their own copies of "The Star-Spangled Banner" to sing in the parlor, they also enjoyed hearing it performed by others. Newspapers of the period regularly announced the song as a feature of concerts, plays, and other entertainments. In October 1815, for example, the Thespian Benevolent Society sang "the justly admired songs of 'The Star-Spangled Banner,' 'My Deary,' and 'Young Lobski'" at the close of a performance in Washington, D.C. The song was also performed in the nation's capital by a Mr. Twibill, in concert with the U.S. Marine Band, in 1819. After a comedic play in Louisville, Kentucky, in 1822, "The Star-Spangled Banner" was followed by "Auld Lang Syne." In 1845 the *New York Herald* reported on a benefit concert at which the "national air, 'The Star-Spangled Banner,' was most beautifully sung." The paper went on to note that the song "is most difficult to sing well, but it was, on this occasion, sung in a manner to excite the warmest feelings of admiration." Others who made the brave attempt included Tom Thumb, the "celebrated man in miniature," who performed "The Star-Spangled Banner" in Cleveland in 1856 while dressed as the Mexican War hero General Winfield Scott.[10]

In addition to earning a place on the popular stage, "The Star-Spangled Banner" also became a standard for patriotic celebrations in the decades before the Civil War. These included national holidays, such as Independence Day and Washington's Birthday, as well as local occasions. In 1817 the anthem was sung at the Tammany Society's annual Evacuation Day banquet, marking the permanent withdrawal of British forces from New York on November 25, 1783. In the tradition of the times, society members drank a series of toasts, accompanied by songs, and "The Star-Spangled Banner" was proposed in honor of "our military and naval heroes of the Revolution and the late War." The following year, the Tammany Society sang the anthem again, this time in tribute to "our flag—stripes and stars: the stripes for the traitor, the stars to illumine the patriot's path to glory." For the seventy-fifth anniversary of American independence in July 1851, the City of Cleveland presented a program of oratory and music, including "The Star-Spangled Banner" and "Hail Columbia," followed by "a magnificent display of fireworks" and hot-air balloon ascensions.[11]

Through shared experiences such as concert performances and holiday celebrations, Americans used "The Star-Spangled Banner" to express their national identity and show their patriotism. Yet as Key's song grew in popularity, it also became a vehicle for other types of political expression. In 1837 the *New-Hampshire Statesman and State Journal* published a revised version of the anthem under the title "A Whig Song," with the third stanza changed to include a reference to "Van Buren corruption" and the conclusion changed to "Then conquer we must! / The WHIG CAUSE is just!"[12] Three years later the Whig party published a songbook, *The Harrison Medal Minstrel,* which contained no fewer than eight songs extolling the virtues of presidential candidate William Henry Harrison to be sung to the tune of "The

Personalizing the Anthem

Since "The Star-Spangled Banner" became the official U.S. national anthem in 1931, musicians have developed their own renditions to appeal to their fans, to make a political statement, or to promote their artistic visions. Artists known for putting their distinctive musical stamp on the song include Igor Stravinsky, José Feliciano, and Jimi Hendrix, as well as many others. While these stylized, unconventional versions sparked controversy, they also garnered critical acclaim and popular success, and they represent significant contributions to American music as well as memorable episodes in the history of the national anthem. In adapting Francis Scott Key's song to fit changing times and tastes, these artists gave new life to an old tradition and inspired Americans—performers and listeners alike—to claim the anthem as their own.

January 14, 1944. Igor Stravinsky (opposite left) conducts his own arrangement of "The Star-Spangled Banner" with the Boston Symphony Orchestra. The Russian-born composer, who had sought refuge in the United States on the eve of World War II, created his version for male chorus in 1941 to "express my gratitude at the prospect of becoming an American citizen" and "do my bit in these grievous times toward fostering and preserving the spirit of patriotism." Audience reaction to Stravinsky's modernist harmonies was mixed, however, and the composer refrained from repeating the performance in Boston after authorities informed him of a Massachusetts law that prohibited "embellishment" of the national anthem.[1]

October 7, 1968. In Detroit, Michigan, singer-songwriter José Feliciano (opposite center) performs a bluesy, folk-rock rendition of "The Star-Spangled Banner" to kick off Game Five of the World Series. The young artist from Puerto Rico, who had overcome obstacles of poverty and blindness to achieve international fame as a pop singer, intended his song to be "an anthem of gratitude" to the United States. He was also eager for the opportunity to express his patriotism in style, to "put some soul" into the old standard. While his rendition drew complaints from baseball fans who were expecting to hear the anthem sung in the traditional way, many others were moved by Feliciano's version, and the recording became a popular hit, reaching No. 50 on the *Billboard* singles chart.[2]

August 18, 1969. On this final morning of the Wood-stock Music and Art Fair, rock guitarist Jimi Hendrix (above right) wakes up the crowd with an electrified ren-dition of "The Star-Spangled Banner." Embraced by fans as "mind-blowing," Hendrix's version, with its distorted explosions of sound, was interpreted by some critics as an antiwar parody. When later asked why he chose to include the national anthem in his set, Hendrix replied, "Because we're all American." He went on to defend his remake of the song as expressing the spirit of the times: "We don't play it to take away all the greatness that America's sup-posed to have. We play it the way the air is in America today. The air is slightly static, isn't it?"[3]

Star-Spangled Banner." Campaign songbooks in every subsequent presidential campaign until the Civil War included songs set to the tune.

In recounting the story of Francis Scott Key and "The Star-Spangled Banner," some critics and historians have noted the irony that a song celebrating "the land of the free" was written by a man who owned slaves. Key grew up in a slaveholding family and maintained a large number of slaves both at his country plantation in Frederick, Maryland, and his residence in Georgetown. In 1838, in response to questions from an abolitionist minister, the devoutly religious Key contended that slavery was morally acceptable as long as slaveholders treated their slaves with kindness, and he expressed his belief that blacks were "a distinct and inferior race." Key opposed abolition but supported colonization, the sending of emancipated slaves to Africa. He maintained this position until his death in 1843.[13]

In the years leading up to the Civil War, Key's song provided unintended inspiration for abolitionists, who used the anthem extensively as a form of social protest. Throughout the 1840s, antislavery newspapers published variations on "The Star-Spangled Banner" that condemned the hypocrisy of American slaveholders. One version, printed by the *Emancipator and Free American* in 1841, asked: "O say, does that blood-striped banner still wave / O'er the land of the fetter, and hut of the slave?" Another, written by E. A. Atlee and published in *The North Star* in 1848, began: "Oh say, do ye hear, at the dawn's early light, / The shrieks of

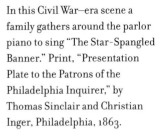

In this Civil War–era scene a family gathers around the parlor piano to sing "The Star-Spangled Banner." Print, "Presentation Plate to the Patrons of the Philadelphia Inquirer," by Thomas Sinclair and Christian Inger, Philadelphia, 1863.

HOW SLAVERY HONORS OUR COUNTRY'S FLAG.

"How Slavery Honors Our Country's Flag." Engraving from *The Anti-slavery Record*, published 1835–1837. Abolitionists composed their own versions of "The Star-Spangled Banner" to challenge the existence of slavery in the "land of the free."

51

those Bondmen, whose blood is now streaming, / From the merciless lash, while our banner in sight, / With its stars mocking Freedom, is fitfully gleaming!"[14]

Temperance activists comprised another group of nineteenth-century reformers who altered Key's song to make a moral point. In 1843 the *Cold Water Magazine* published a parody that began: "Oh! Who has not seen, by the dawn's early light / Some poor bloated drunkard to his home weakly reeling / With blear eyes and red nose most revolting to sight / Yet still in his breast not a throb of shame feeling?" A more hopeful view was expressed in a version by C. W. Appleton, published in 1841: "Oh, say, can you see, by the 'signs of the times,' / That men are reforming, themselves setting free / From all that destroys their bodies and minds, / Resolving to plant a new liberty tree." The stanza concluded, "For the TEMPERANCE BANNER in triumph doth wave, / O'er the heads of the rescued, free sons of the brave."[15]

These examples suggest that by the 1840s "The Star-Spangled Banner" had become popular enough to make its tune an attractive vehicle for parody. The song's popularity increased enormously during the Civil War, according to Library of Congress scholar Oscar Sonneck and also George J. Svejda, who wrote a detailed history of "The Star-Spangled Banner" for the National Park Service in 1969. Because the song extolled the national flag, which was a symbol of loyalty to the Union, Northerners enthusiastically embraced it as a patriotic anthem. It was performed at public appearances of President and Mrs. Abraham Lincoln. It was played by countless military bands and sung, both as a solo and in chorus, on hundreds of other occasions in the North. It was the music to which Union armies entered New Orleans, Savannah, Richmond, and many other Southern towns. It was even played in the trenches, as described by Lieutenant S. Millett Thompson, a soldier with the Thirteenth New Hampshire, after the second Battle of Cold Harbor, Virginia, in June 1864:

> This evening the Band of the Thirteenth goes into the trenches at the front, and indulges in a "competition concert" with a band that is playing over across in the enemy's trenches. The enemy's Band renders Dixie, Bonnie Blue Flag, My Maryland, and other airs dear to the Southerner's heart. Our Band replies with America, Star Spangled Banner, Old John Brown, etc. After a little time, the enemy's band introduces another class of music; only to be joined almost instantly by our Band with the same tune. All at once the band over there stops, and a rebel battery opens with grape. Very few of our men are exposed, so the enemy wasted his ammunition; while our band continues its playing, all the more earnestly until all their shelling is over.[16]

Long after the Civil War was over, hundreds of thousands of Union veterans continued to associate the tune with the excitement and emotion of their wartime experiences.

In the 1890s and the early 1900s, as the United States expanded into a leading economic and military power, a surge of nationalistic sentiment gave Francis Scott Key's song a boost toward a more official status. The first formal step in that direction was taken in 1889 by the secretary of the navy, Benjamin F. Tracy, who issued orders requiring that "The Star-Spangled Banner" be played by all navy bands at morning colors, the ceremony at which the flag was raised each day. The next year Secretary Tracy ordered the U.S. Marine Band to play it at the close of their public performances. The band's annual national tours, initiated in 1891, did much to reinforce the song's popularity. In 1895 army regulations made the tune the prescribed music to be played as the flag was lowered at evening colors, and in 1904 the navy amended its regulations to include both morning and evening colors. In 1903 the navy issued General Order No. 139, which required all officers and men to stand at attention while "The Star-Spangled Banner" was played. The army issued a similar regulation in 1904. Reflecting the militaristic spirit that pervaded popular culture during this period, civilian audiences adopted this custom as well and began standing for the song at theaters and baseball games. In 1917 both the army and the navy designated "The Star-Spangled Banner" as "the national anthem of the United States" for ceremonial purposes.[17]

Congressional recognition of the song as a national anthem, however, did not come until 1931. Although the Daughters of the American Revolution discussed petitioning Congress to make such a designation as early as 1897, the first bill to do so was not introduced until 1912, by Congressman George Edmond Foss of Illinois. It failed to reach the floor of the House, as did fifteen subsequent bills and resolutions introduced between 1912 and 1917. As Congressman George Murray Hulbert of New York told Alfred J. Carr, the president of the Maryland

"Elmira Cornet Band," Thirty-third Regiment of the New York State Volunteers, July 1861.

A translation of Francis Scott Key's lyrics for German immigrants, thousands of whom fought for the Union during the Civil War. Published by H. De Marsan, New York, circa 1861–1865.

Service version of "The Star-Spangled Banner," published by Oliver Ditson, Boston, 1918. During World War I the War Department established a standard instrumental arrangement to be used by U.S. military bands. Although this arrangement is often used in nonmilitary performances, there is no single official version of the anthem designated for civilian use.

Israel Fine, a Russian Jewish immigrant living in Baltimore, made this embroidered silk scroll cover in 1914 in honor of the one hundredth anniversary of the composition of "The Star-Spangled Banner." Resembling a mantle for a Torah, it features an inscription in Hebrew, "The flag of Judah," and the U.S. motto, E Pluribus Unum, "Out of many, one." Inside is a scroll with a patriotic hymn in Hebrew and English written by Fine.

Society of the War of 1812, there was simply not enough public interest in the matter to goad Congress into action.

In 1918, Mrs. Reuben Ross Holloway, president of the Maryland State Society, United States Daughters of 1812, joined forces with Congressman J. Charles Linthicum of Baltimore to press for congressional recognition of the song as the national anthem. A series of bills introduced by Linthicum between 1918 and 1927 died in committee. But in 1929, Holloway succeeded in gaining support for the next Linthicum bill from various patriotic organizations. The bill making "The Star-Spangled Banner" the national anthem of the United States passed both the House and the Senate and was signed into law by President Herbert Hoover on March 3, 1931.[18]

ONE VERSE, MANY VOICES

As the national anthem, "The Star-Spangled Banner" has become a cherished tradition in American life—played at official ceremonies, sung at sporting events, and performed by school bands. Yet like the flag, the song has also sparked its share of controversy over the years. Many have criticized it for being too difficult to sing. Some have disqualified it as a truly national song because the original melody is British, not American. Others have condemned the lyrics for expressing anti-British feelings or for glorifying war. While calling attention to the faults of "The Star-Spangled Banner," many have also promoted other popular patriotic songs—such as Irving Berlin's "God Bless America" or "America, the Beautiful," written by Katharine Lee Bates—as being more appropriate for the title of national anthem.

In addition to debating whether we have picked the right national anthem, Americans have often struggled to define the right way to perform it. The bill establishing "The Star-Spangled Banner" as the national anthem made no reference to how much of the song should be sung or in what key, tempo, or style. In fact, the bill consisted of just a single sentence: "Be it enacted by the Senate and House of Representatives of the United States of America, in Congress assembled, that the composition consisting of the words and music known as 'The Star-Spangled Banner' is designated the national anthem of the United States of America." The language of the original 1931 bill is retained today in the U.S. Code, Title 36, Section 301: "The composition consisting of the words and music known as the Star-Spangled Banner is the national anthem." While the U.S. Code does specify proper conduct for audiences during the playing of the anthem—individuals should stand facing the flag, if it is displayed, with their right hands over their hearts—it does not offer similar guidance to performers.

The lack of laws regarding the proper performance of the national anthem does not represent a lack of trying, however. In 1957, at the request of Joel T. Broyhill, congressman from Virginia, the National Music Council developed a proposal for an official version of "The Star-Spangled Banner." Along with setting standards for the words, melody, rhythm, and harmony, the council proposed general guidelines for how the song should be played: "The anthem should always be performed in a manner that gives it due honor and respect.

The custom of standing for "The Star-Spangled Banner" began at military ceremonies in the 1890s. Since then, Americans have expressed their feelings for the flag by standing for the national anthem—or by choosing not to.

It should never be performed as part of a medley or in circumstances where its importance as a national symbol is in any way cheapened. Its use to build dramatic effects, wholly subsidiary to its fundamental purpose, should be discouraged."[19] Despite the efforts of Broyhill and others, though, no bill providing for a standardized version of the national anthem has ever passed in Congress. Like those who have tried to prohibit desecration of the American flag, citizens who have aimed to protect "The Star-Spangled Banner" from musical abuse have faced resistance from those who believe diverse interpretations of the national song—whether artistic or political, in tune or off-key—are symbolic of an essential right to free expression.

Following the death of Francis Scott Key in January 1843, the *Baltimore American* paid tribute to the creator of "The Star-Spangled Banner," proclaiming, "So long as patriotism dwells among us, so long will this song be the theme of our nation." This prediction has come true, in ways the newspaper writer could never have imagined. But even then the song elicited mixed feelings from the American people, as it still does today. Like many expressions of patriotism, the national anthem evokes pride in American ideals while also provoking debate about the meaning and pursuit of those ideals. Those contradictions were originally embodied by Key himself: an opponent of war who glorified a military victory; a slaveholder who created a paean to freedom. Because it resonated with national ideas, emotions, and conflicts, "The Star-Spangled Banner" transcended its origins as a song about a single battle and came to play an enduring and powerful role in American life. In many vital respects, for the ways it unites us and also illuminates our differences, it is indeed the theme of our nation.

Ambrotype portrait. Wrapped in camp blankets with the flag nestled between them as if it were an old comrade, these Union soldiers expressed the loyalty and affection many Civil War veterans held for the national emblem.

MEANINGS AND MEMORIES   THE FLAG

Nearly fifty years after Francis Scott Key immortalized the victorious flag of Fort McHenry, another American flag was lowered in defeat after Confederate forces captured the federal garrison in Charleston harbor. The attack on Fort Sumter in April 1861 launched the nation into civil war and brought about lasting changes in how Americans viewed and used the Star-Spangled Banner. Through Key's song, an earlier generation had come to appreciate the flag's value as an inspiring and unifying national symbol. The Civil War not only revived that patriotic attachment to the flag but expanded and intensified it, fostering a spirit of reverence and devotion that would endure for generations to come. Entwined with a war to redefine the United States and

what it should stand for, the flag became the primary icon of national identity and ideals, infused with meanings and memories from all sides of the conflict.

For Northerners who were called upon to defend the Union created by the founding fathers, the flag became the sacred emblem of that cause, consecrated in battle by the blood of Union soldiers. The banner took on heightened meaning when, in his 1863 Gettysburg Address, President Abraham Lincoln identified the war's true purpose: not only to save the Union, but to secure a "new birth of freedom" for the nation. With the abolition of slavery and the opening of the Union ranks to black soldiers, many African Americans saw the flag in a new light, as

FAR LEFT

Recruitment handbill. After the Union army opened its ranks to them in 1863, African American soldiers fought under the flag to gain their freedom and secure equal rights of citizenship.

LEFT

Lincoln campaign ribbon. A moderate Republican, Abraham Lincoln opposed the expansion of slavery into the territories. But in hopes of preserving the Union, he pledged to uphold the Constitution's protection of slavery in the states. Southern states rejected this compromise, however, and responded to Lincoln's victory in 1860 by seceding from the Union and setting the stage for civil war.

IN THE CIVIL WAR

a symbol of freedom and the promise of citizenship. For members of the Southern Confederacy, meanwhile, the "old flag" they had once loved had come to stand for a federal government that did not respect their rights and threatened their way of life. In taking up arms against the Star-Spangled Banner, they projected their patriotism onto a new national flag, one that embodied American values as they defined them.

The artifacts and images on these pages reflect how the Civil War transformed the American flag into a sacred symbol worth defending and dying for—on the battlefield and beyond. In February 1865, Private John N. Sherman of the First New York Artillery drew inspiration from Francis Scott Key's lyrics when he

promised his parents: "We shall come forth from the fire of trial and have proven to the world that . . . our country is indeed the land of the free and the home of the brave." The ultimate defeat of the Confederacy ensured that the Union, and its flag, would survive. Yet in the struggle to transform the American flag into a symbol of freedom and equality for all, the Civil War was only the first of many battles yet to come.[1]

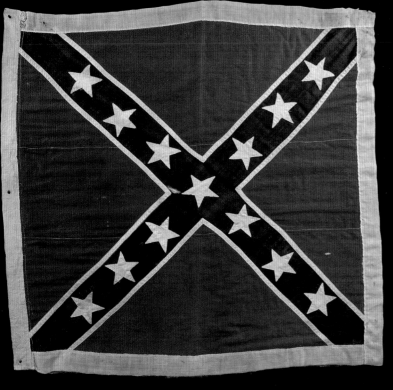

Confederate battle flag. The first
Confederate national flag, known
as the "Stars and Bars," often
proved indistinguishable from the
"Stars and Stripes" in the thick
of battle. This led in the fall of 1861
to the creation of the battle flag,
a square red field with a blue,
star-studded "Southern Cross,"
which became the icon of the
Confederacy.

**"Farewell to the Star-Spangled
Banner."** Confederate sheet music
published in Richmond, Virginia,
circa 1861.

Stars-and-stripes quilt. On the
home front many women supported the war effort by making
flags and domestic items for the
troops. Mary Rockhold Teter of
Noblesville, Indiana, made this
patriotic bed quilt for her soldier
son using a pattern published in
Peterson's Magazine in July 1861.

Pennsylvania Academy of Fine Arts students with handmade flag. Photograph by John Moran, 1862.

The original "Old Glory." Made in 1824 for Captain William Driver, who gave it the name "Old Glory" when it flew from his ship during his sailing days, this flag was hoisted over the state capitol in Nashville, Tennessee, after Union forces recaptured the city in February 1862. The widely told story of Driver and his flag—which he had hidden from the Confederates by sewing it inside a quilt—popularized "Old Glory" as a name for all American flags.

MAKING THE FLAG

A most superb and splendid ensign . . .

—British midshipman Robert Barrett, describing the Star-Spangled Banner, 1843

The flag that so impressed and inspired Francis Scott Key on the morning of September 14, 1814, was made for Fort McHenry under a government contract by a Baltimore flagmaker, Mary Pickersgill, in the summer of 1813.

After receiving his orders to take command of the fort on June 27, 1813, Major George Armistead continued the improvements to the fort's defenses that Major General Samuel Smith had initiated that spring, after the British fleet began taking menacing action in the Chesapeake Bay region. Armistead also posted a recruitment notice in the local papers seeking "reputable young men" to expand the fort's understaffed garrison. Soon after his arrival Armistead reported to Smith on his progress: "We, Sir, are ready at Fort McHenry to defend Baltimore against invading by the enemy. . . . Except that we have no suitable ensign to display over the Star Fort [Fort McHenry], and it is my desire to have a flag so large that the British will have no difficulty in seeing it from a distance." At about that same time someone, probably James Calhoun, the U.S. Army's deputy commissary officer in Baltimore, ordered two flags from Mary Pickersgill: a garrison flag, thirty by forty-two feet, and a smaller storm flag, seventeen by twenty-five feet. Although it seems large today, the garrison flag was a standard size for the time, about

Detail of the Star-Spangled Banner.

one-fourth the size of a modern basketball court. Garrison flags were intended to fly over forts on flagpoles as high as ninety feet and to be seen from great distances. Armistead seems to have had a special fondness for large flags: when he was stationed at Fort Niagara in 1802, he had requested a flag thirty-six feet wide and forty-eight feet long.[1]

The Fort McHenry flags were delivered to the fort on August 19, 1813. On October 27, Pickersgill received $405.90 for the large flag and $168.54 for the smaller one—a considerable sum of money at the time. The receipt for payment, endorsed on the reverse by Major Armistead and signed for by Pickersgill's niece, Eliza Young, is in the collection of the Flag House and Star-Spangled Banner Museum, the site of Pickersgill's former home in Baltimore.

"AN EXCEEDINGLY PATRIOTIC WOMAN"

Born in Philadelphia on February 12, 1776, Mary Young Pickersgill was an experienced flagmaker who had learned the art from her mother, Rebecca Flower Young. Mary's father, William Young, died when she was two years old, and Rebecca supported herself and her children by making blankets, uniforms, and flags for George Washington's Continental army. After the war the Young family moved to Baltimore. On October 2, 1795, Mary married John Pickersgill, a Baltimore merchant. The couple moved to Philadelphia, where they lived until John Pickersgill's death in 1805, after which Mary returned to Baltimore with her daughter, Caroline, and went into business making flags with her mother. Advertising their services in local newspapers, Rebecca Young and her daughter offered "Colors of every description" from the family home at the corner of Albemarle and Pratt streets, located a few blocks from the harbor.[2]

Most of Mary Pickersgill's orders were for ships' colors and signal flags, flown by the numerous military and merchant vessels that sailed in and out of Baltimore's busy port. According to Pickersgill's daughter, the Fort McHenry commission was facilitated by "family connections" to two men who played prominent roles in Baltimore's defense during the War of 1812: Commodore Joshua Barney and General John Stricker. Barney, Stricker, and Mary's uncle John Young had all married daughters of Philadelphia architect Gunning Bedford. In making the enormous garrison flag, Pickersgill was helped by her thirteen-year-old daughter Caroline, her teenaged nieces Eliza and Margaret Young, and a young African American indentured servant, Grace Wisher, who was apprenticed in 1809 to spend six years learning "the art and mystery of Housework and plain sewing" from Pickersgill.[3] Rebecca Young, then seventy-three years old, may have assisted her daughter as well.

Historical and physical evidence reveals that the techniques used to make the Star-Spangled Banner were typical of the period. Pickersgill's receipt for the Fort McHenry flags notes that they were made of "first quality Bunting," a specialized type of worsted wool manufactured in England.[4] The wool was colored with natural dyes—indigo for the blue union (also called the canton), madder with tin mordant for the red stripes. The stars, made of cotton,

Mary Pickersgill, maker of the Star-Spangled Banner. Portrait by P. L. Pickens, circa 1850.

were sewn into the union by reverse appliqué method, in which each star was stitched into place on one side of the flag and the cloth on the other side was then cut away to reveal it. Each star is about two feet across, and each stripe is about twenty-three inches wide. Since the bunting was not woven wider than eighteen inches, a complete width and a partial width were sewn together to produce each stripe.

To finish the flag, a linen sleeve was sewn to the hoist, the part closest to the pole. A length of rope with iron rings, or thimbles, could be passed through the sleeve, allowing the flag to be attached to a halyard and raised on a flagpole. When repairs were made to the Star-Spangled Banner later on, the hoist edge was folded over and the sleeve relocated further

Receipt given to Mary Pickersgill by the U.S. Army for making the Star-Spangled Banner, 1813.

into the flag. In 1914 flag preservationist Amelia Fowler removed the hoist rope when she remounted the Star-Spangled Banner for display at the Smithsonian. Stored away for nearly a century, the hoist rope was recently reattached to the flag, restoring a long-forgotten piece of its history.

More than sixty years after she helped her mother make the flag, Caroline Pickersgill Purdy wrote a letter to George Armistead's daughter, Georgiana Armistead Appleton, who had inherited the Star-Spangled Banner and was planning to lend it to the 1876 Philadelphia Centennial Exhibition. Purdy noted that her mother had readily accepted the commission to make the Fort McHenry flag, "being an exceedingly patriotic woman." She recalled the hours they had spent sewing the enormous flag: "The flag being so very large, my mother was obliged to obtain permission from the proprietors of Claggetts brewery, which was in our neighborhood, to spread it out in their malt house; and I remember seeing my mother down on the floor, placing the stars. . . . The flag contained, I think, four hundred yards of bunting, and my mother worked many nights until 12 o'clock to complete it in the given time."[5]

The fact that Mary Pickersgill worked late into the night to complete the flag reflected the urgent circumstances that compelled the making of the Star-Spangled Banner during the summer of 1813. In late July, shortly after Armistead took command of Fort McHenry, the city was gripped by the fear of an impending attack when the British fleet began sailing up the Chesapeake Bay toward Baltimore. Major General Smith put the militia on full alert, instituting daily drills and cavalry patrols of the area surrounding the city. "Our Enemy is at

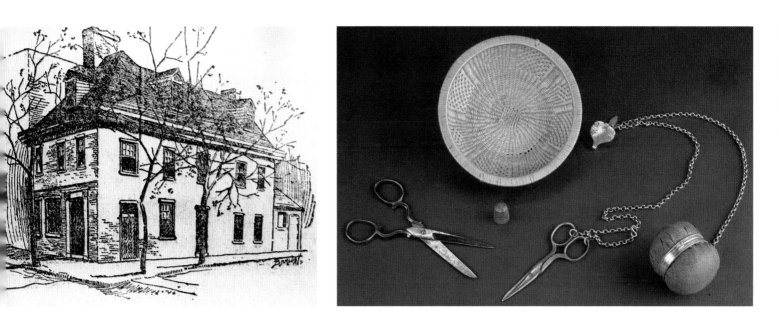

the door," declared Captain John H. Rogers, calling up his Fifty-first Regiment of Baltimore militia; "therefore it is hoped that no Man, who wishes well to his Country, will be missing."[6] On August 8 the British ships reappeared at the mouth of the Patapsco River. For three long weeks they anchored there, blockading the port and keeping residents in taut suspense.

Pickersgill delivered the flags to Fort McHenry on August 19, 1813, just before the British fleet weighed anchor on August 24 and departed for winter quarters in the West Indies. It would be another year before the British returned to Baltimore and the garrison flag achieved its historic moment of glory. But thanks to the quick fingers of Pickersgill and her assistants, who in a matter of weeks had managed to complete the gigantic banner that could be seen for miles around, the city had a new symbol of pride and defiance to wave. Hoisted over the ramparts of Fort McHenry by Major Armistead and his men, the flag sent a signal to friend and foe alike that the people of Baltimore were willing and ready to defend themselves.

TATTERED AND TORN

Over the years many observers have assumed that the damage to the Star-Spangled Banner was primarily caused by enemy bombs and rockets fired on Fort McHenry in September 1814. When historian Benson J. Lossing visited the home of George Armistead's son, Christopher Hughes Armistead, in 1861, he examined the famous flag and found "eleven holes in it, made there by the shot of the British during the bombardment."[7] Yet in the 1972 book *By the Dawn's Early Light*, popular historian Walter Lord raised an important question based on the eyewitness accounts of midshipman Robert Barrett and private Isaac Munroe, both of whom described a flag being hoisted over the fort on the morning of September 14. Lord suggested that the smaller storm flag that Mary Pickersgill made might have been flown over the fort

Mary Pickersgill's house in Baltimore, where the Star-Spangled Banner was made in 1813. This sketch shows the house as it appeared in the 1890s; converted to a museum by the Star-Spangled Banner Flag House Association in 1927, it still stands today.

Early-nineteenth-century sewing implements—chatelaine with scissors and pin cushion, larger scissors, thimble, and sewing basket—of the type Mary Pickersgill and her assistants might have used to make the Star-Spangled Banner.

What about Betsy Ross?

Many visitors who come to the National Museum of American History to see the original Star-Spangled Banner ask the inevitable question: Did Betsy Ross make this flag? The answer, of course, is no—Mary Pickersgill, a Baltimore flagmaker, made the flag for Fort McHenry in 1813. But the fact that Americans commonly associate Betsy Ross with the making of early flags reflects the enduring appeal of a popular legend that first emerged more than a century ago.

In 1870 Ross's grandson, William J. Canby, presented a paper to the Historical Society of Pennsylvania in which he claimed that his grandmother, a Quaker widow who operated an upholstery shop in Philadelphia during the Revolution, had "made with her hands the first flag" of the United States. Canby recounted the story that he had first heard from his aunt Clarissa Wilson in 1857, twenty years after Betsy Ross's death:

> Sitting sewing in her shop one day with her girls around her, several gentlemen entered. She recognized one of these as the uncle of her deceased husband, Colonel George Ross, a delegate from Pennsylvania to Congress. She also knew the handsome form and features of the dignified, yet graceful and polite Commander in Chief, who, while he was yet Colonel Washington had visited her shop both professionally and socially many times (a friendship caused by her connection with the Ross family). They announced themselves as a committee of congress, and stated that they had been appointed to prepare a flag, and asked her if she thought she could make one, to which she replied, with her usual modesty and self reliance, that "she did not know but she could try; she had never made one but if the pattern were shown to her she had no doubt of her ability to do it." The committee was shown into her back parlor, the room back of the shop, and Colonel Ross produced a drawing, roughly made, of the proposed flag. It was defective to the clever eye of Mrs. Ross and unsymmetrical, and she offered suggestions which Washington and the committee readily approved. . . . One of the alterations had reference to the shape of the stars. In the drawing they were made with six points. Mrs. Ross at once said that this was wrong; the stars should be five pointed; they were aware of that, but thought there would be some difficulty in making a five pointed star. "Nothing easier" was her prompt reply, and folding a piece of paper in the proper manner, with one clip of her ready scissors she quickly displayed to their astonished vision the five pointed star, which accordingly took its place in the national standard.[1]

The Birth of Our Nation's Flag,
by Charles H. Weisgerber.
Originally painted for the 1893
World's Columbian Exposition
in Chicago, this imaginary scene
of Betsy Ross presenting the
first flag to George Washington
was often reproduced in history
textbooks and helped to establish the Betsy Ross myth in the
American popular imagination.

This historic episode supposedly occurred in late May or early June of 1776, a year before Congress passed the Flag Act.

Brought to light as the United States prepared to celebrate its one hundredth anniversary of independence, Canby's romantic tale appealed to Americans eager for stories about the Revolution and its heroes. As one of only a few recognized Revolutionary heroines, Betsy Ross was promoted as a patriotic role model for young girls and a symbol of women's contributions to American history.

Betsy Ross was in fact a professional flagmaker—one of many women, including Mary Pickersgill's mother, who practiced that trade during the War of Independence—and she did make a set of flags for Pennsylvania state ships in 1777. But historians have found no documentary evidence to support the claim that she made the very first Stars and Stripes at George Washington's request. Nevertheless, the legend has been repeated often in print and even in textbooks, and remains popular today—a cherished myth that has its own place in American history.[2]

"Admiral Cockburn Burning and Plundering Havre de Grace [Maryland]." Print by William Charles, Philadelphia, circa 1813. As the British navy terrorized towns along the Chesapeake Bay during the summer of 1813, Baltimore's defenders prepared Fort McHenry for attack.

during the wet and windy night of the bombardment and the larger flag substituted for it in the morning. This would have been consistent with military practice of the time.[8]

But another eyewitness, Mendes I. Cohen, who was in the fort as an eighteen-year-old member of Joseph Nicholson's volunteer company, offers a contradictory account. He wrote in 1873: "I have a full recollection of the damage to the flag by the enemy. . . . I have a recollection that one whole bomb shell passed through it and some three or four pieces passed through it. The flag was on a high mast not far from the bastion I was stationed at on the right side of the star fort. . . . I do not recollect the size of the flag tho I know it was a very large one and have only seen it once since then in the possession of Mr. Hughes Armistead the brother of Mrs. Appleton."[9] In her 1876 letter to Georgiana Armistead Appleton, Caroline Pickersgill Purdy also asserted that the Star-Spangled Banner had flown during the bombardment, with "many shots piercing it, but it still remained firm to the staff." She recalled that Major Armistead asked her mother to repair the battle-scarred banner: "Your father declared that no one but the maker of the flag should mend it, and requested that the rents be merely bound round."[10]

In light of conflicting evidence from witnesses, can any clues be drawn from the Star-Spangled Banner itself? During the preservation project conservators thoroughly examined the flag and documented its condition. They identified nearly two hundred heavily damaged areas that had been mended or patched over time. The largest hole, located in the center of the Star-Spangled Banner where the fifteenth star once was, would seem consistent with Cohen's account of seeing a British bombshell burst through the flag. Family history reveals that the missing star was not taken by a bomb, however, but cut out by Armistead's widow to give away as an honored memento. Although the cotton fibers of the remaining stars show some indications of exposure to battle conditions, there is no physical evidence anywhere on the flag of direct hits from enemy fire. In fact, many smaller holes that had been traditionally attributed to shot and shrapnel were determined to be the result of insect damage. Since the garrison flag had flown at Fort McHenry for more than a year before the battle, some repairs also might have been made during that early period, as part of the routine care of a valuable piece of military equipment. Overall, the conservators' findings suggest that most of the damage and loss to the Star-Spangled Banner did not occur during the battle itself.

But what to make of Mendes Cohen's "full recollection" of seeing the large garrison flag flying during the bombardment? Although smaller than the Star-Spangled Banner, the storm flag, at seventeen by twenty-five feet, was still of a considerable size. Its height against the flagpole was not much greater than that of present-day army garrison flags, which are set at a standard twenty by thirty-six feet. Thus it is possible that the flag Cohen saw pierced by a

Details of the Star-Spangled Banner, showing some of its many patches and mends.

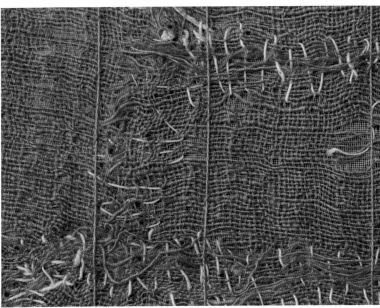

A 1796 hand-colored flagsheet by Vincenzo Scotti of Livorno, Italy, includes seven different versions of the American flag observed on U.S. merchant and naval ships of the period.

British bombshell was the storm flag, rather than the garrison flag. The smaller flag, unfortunately, has never been located.

STARS AND STRIPES

The design of the flag that Mary Pickersgill and her family made for Fort McHenry in 1813, with fifteen stars and fifteen stripes, was the second official version of the American flag. The original Flag Act, passed June 14, 1777, provided that "the flag of the thirteen United States be thirteen stripes, alternate red and white; that the union be thirteen stars, white in a blue field, representing a new constellation." Credit for the basic design of the first U.S. flag is often given to Francis Hopkinson, a New Jersey delegate to the Continental Congress, member of the Continental Navy Board, composer, and designer of several government seals. In May 1780, Hopkinson submitted the first of several bills to the Continental Congress for designing the Board of Admiralty seal, the Treasury Board seal, the Great Seal of the United States, a number of devices and ornaments for treasury bills and ships' papers, and "the Flag of the United States." The bills became part of a bureaucratic battle between the Congress, the Auditor General, and the Board of Treasury. Eventually the Board of Treasury had the last word, denying Hopkinson payment on the grounds that the public was entitled to expect extra services from officials who drew high salaries and that Hopkinson "was not the only person consulted on these [designs] . . . and therefore cannot claim the sole merit of them and is not entitled to the full sum charged."[11]

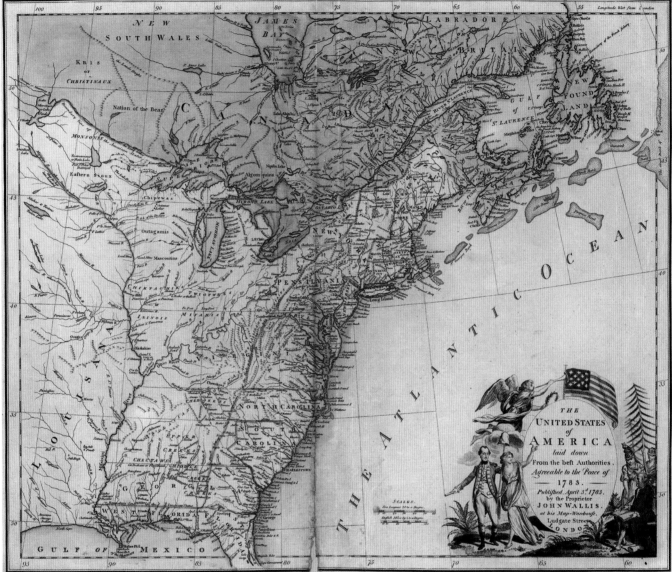

At only thirty-one words the Flag Act of 1777 did not do much more than establish the colors and essential elements of the flag. The placement of neither the stripes nor the stars was specified, and a wide variety of designs appeared during the early years of the Republic. In some the blue union ran down the entire hoist of the flag; others mixed blue stripes in with the red and white, creating a tricolor effect. Similarly, in deciding how to arrange the thirteen stars, individual flagmakers developed different kinds of "constellations." Although most Americans today think of a thirteen-star flag in the circular "Betsy Ross" pattern, in reality this was not the only design used during the Revolutionary period. Often the stars

Map of the United States of America. Published by John Wallis, London, 1783. On the decorative title cartouche of this map, created at the end of the War of Independence, the thirteen stars on the U.S. flag appear in symmetrical rows.

73

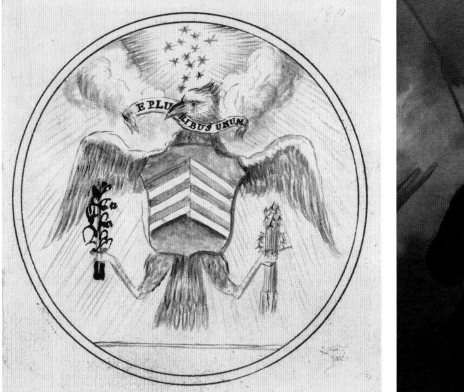

Charles Thomson's design for the Great Seal of the United States. After minor revisions by William Barton, including changing the chevrons on the shield to vertical stripes, this design was approved by Congress on June 20, 1782.

Captain Samuel Chester Reid, naval hero of the War of 1812 and redesigner of the U.S. flag. Reid's proposal to have thirteen permanent stripes for the original colonies, with a changing number of stars to represent the current number of states, was the inspiration for the third Flag Act, passed by Congress in 1818. Portrait by John Wesley Jarvis, 1815.

appeared in rows, which was a much simpler pattern to produce. Another design, documented in images from the era, placed twelve stars in a square, with the thirteenth star in the center.

Although Francis Scott Key would later draw his inspiration from the stars that spangled the flag, the stripes carried more symbolic significance during the American Revolution. Stripes first appeared as a sign of colonial rebellion in the 1760s, when the Sons of Liberty flew flags with nine alternate red and white stripes from "Liberty poles" to protest British taxation. In January 1776, General George Washington rallied his Continental troops by raising a "Union flag," which combined a canton containing the British crosses of St. George and St. Andrew with thirteen horizontal stripes representing the united colonies. But this mixture of American and British elements caused confusion, according to Washington, who noted that the raising of the flag "was received in Boston . . . as a signal of submission" to the king, rather than an expression of colonial solidarity.[12]

While the number of stars and stripes clearly represented the thirteen original states, the Flag Act did not define the meaning of the flag's colors. Five years later, when presenting the design for the Great Seal of the United States, Secretary of Congress Charles Thomson discussed the colors shared by the national emblems: "The colours of the pales [vertical stripes on the shield] are those used in the flag of the United States of America. White signifies purity and innocence, Red hardiness and valour, and Blue, the colour of the Chief [top part of the shield], signifies vigilance, perseverance, and justice."[13] Although Thomson's 1782 report mentions the U.S. flag, it was only intended to explain the colors of the Great Seal. What the colors of the flag represent, both individually and together, is not codified by law but open to popular interpretation, and throughout history Americans have ascribed many different meanings to the red, white, and blue.

The fifteen stripes and fifteen stars of the Fort McHenry flag reflected a change introduced by the second Flag Act, which was passed January 13, 1794. The act stipulated that after May 1, 1795, the flag design should acknowledge the two new states—Kentucky and Vermont—that had joined the union since the original Flag Act. The fifteen-star, fifteen-stripe design remained intact from 1794 until 1818, even though additional states continued to join the union after 1795. In 1818, Congressman Peter Wendover of New York introduced a bill based on a proposal from naval captain and War of 1812 hero Samuel Chester Reid. The bill would reduce the number of stripes in the flag to thirteen, intended to signify the original thirteen states. It would increase the number of stars to twenty, the number of existing states, while providing that stars for new states would be added to the flag on the Fourth of July following admission to statehood. President James Monroe signed Wendover's bill into law on April 4, 1818, thereby establishing the fundamental design of the current American flag.

An executive order issued by President William Howard Taft on June 24, 1912, was the first legislation to establish an official arrangement of stars and proportions for the U.S. flag, which was just about to acquire its forty-eighth star. The order specified a ratio of 1:1.9 for the hoist (width) and fly (length), with thirteen stripes of equal width and a union (blue field) seven stripes wide. The forty-eight stars were to be arranged in six horizontal rows of eight, with a single point of each star aimed upward. President Dwight D. Eisenhower revised these regulations in 1959 to provide for the arrangement of forty-nine and then fifty stars on the flag, for Alaska and then Hawaii. Credit for the fifty-star arrangement is often given to Robert Heft, who, as an Ohio high school student in 1958, designed a fifty-star flag as a class project and sent it to Washington, D.C., asking his congressman to submit it for consideration as a future design for the U.S. flag. The same pattern Heft devised, five rows of six stars alternating with four rows of five stars, was later established as the official design in President Eisenhower's executive order of August 21, 1959.[14]

With its fifteen stars and fifteen stripes, the Star-Spangled Banner represents a unique moment in the evolution of the American flag. Between 1777 and 1960 a total of twenty-seven different official versions were created as new states added their stars to the "new constellation." Although the number of stars—and stripes—has changed over time, the flag's power to inspire ideas and emotions about what it means to be American has remained constant from one generation to the next.

MEANINGS AND MEMORIES FLAG

To contemporary Americans, the Armistead family's treatment of the Star-Spangled Banner—marking up the stars and stripes with signatures, cutting off pieces to give away as souvenirs—might seem strange, inappropriate, or even offensive. Today an extensive set of rules, known as the U.S. Flag Code, defines the proper way to treat the American flag. The Pledge of Allegiance, still recited daily in many schools across the country, reflects and reinforces this sense of ceremonial respect for the national symbol. But in fact these rules and customs surrounding the flag date back only to the late nineteenth century.

The U.S. Flag Code

Led by Civil War veterans who wanted to uphold the sacred character of the national emblem they had fought to defend, the first efforts to restrict uses of the flag were targeted at commercial and political advertisements. In 1880, Representative Hiram Barber of Illinois proposed a bill in Congress to make it "unlawful for any person to print, stamp, or in any manner impress upon the flag of the United States, or any representation thereof, any word, figure, design, or impression calculated to serve as an advertisement of merchandise or other property, or of any person's trade, occupation, or business." Although

the federal government did not pass any flag desecration legislation until the 1960s, by the early 1900s most states had adopted such laws, and in 1907 the U.S. Supreme Court upheld a Nebraska statute in a case against a manufacturer of "Stars and Stripes" beer.

The flag-protection movement regained national momentum during World War I, and on June 14, 1923, the first National Flag Conference was held in Washington, D.C., to establish a set of rules for civilian flag use. The U.S. Flag Code, first published in 1923 and adopted by Congress in 1942, is based on the belief that the American flag "represents the living country and is itself considered a living thing." It proscribes any use of the flag that could be construed as disrespectful, including using it for advertising and to decorate clothing and other goods. Although the U.S. Supreme Court struck down flag-protection laws as violations of free speech in 1989, the Flag Code is still maintained as a code of etiquette, enforced not by law but by tradition.[1]

The Pledge of Allegiance

As turn-of-the-century advocates sought to prevent people from misusing the flag, they also created new uses that promoted and reinforced respect for the national emblem. Many of these

RULES AND RITUALS

rituals were geared toward children, to encourage their development into patriotic citizens. Before the 1890s the flag did not have the near universal presence in public schools that it does today; that transformation came about after the Grand Army of the Republic, the largest organization of Civil War veterans, launched a campaign to place a flag in every public school. Once the flag entered the classroom, it became a centerpiece of school activities, including essay assignments, band concerts, holiday pageants, and military-style drills. The idea of a daily salute to the flag also began to take hold. On October 21, 1892, millions of schoolchildren participated in a nationwide celebration to mark the four hundredth anniversary of Christopher Columbus's arrival in the New World. Organized by *The Youth's Companion,* a Boston-based children's magazine, the event featured a program of patriotic activities, including a new Pledge of Allegiance to the flag written by the magazine's associate editor, Francis Bellamy:

> I pledge allegiance to my Flag and the Republic for which it stands: one Nation indivisible, with Liberty and Justice for All.

Over the next century the Pledge of Allegiance became a daily ritual in many public schools. At times it has also provoked controversy. Bellamy's original language was first modified by the National Flag Conference in 1923—"my flag" became "the flag of the United States"—out of concern that immigrant children might envision their native emblem instead of the American flag. (The words "of America" were added the following year at the second flag conference.) The addition of the phrase "under God" in 1954, a Cold War gesture intended to distinguish the religiously tolerant United States from "godless" communist nations, has led some to criticize the pledge as violating the separation of church and state. In 2004 a U.S. Supreme Court case challenging the language provoked resolutions from Congress expressing overwhelming support for retaining the phrase "under God"; the case was ultimately dismissed on a technicality. Meanwhile, although many state and local districts have passed laws requiring the Pledge of Allegiance to be recited daily in classrooms, students also have the right to abstain from participating, according to a 1943 U.S. Supreme Court ruling that still stands today.

Trade card. In an efficient combination of political and commercial advertising, the red and white stripes of this flag promote a dry goods company in Providence, Rhode Island, while the blue canton carries a portrait of General Winfield Scott Hancock, the 1880 Democratic presidential candidate.

McKinley-Roosevelt campaign umbrella. The American flag figured prominently in the 1896 and 1900 presidential campaigns, both of which pitted William McKinley of the Republican Party against Democratic nominee William Jennings Bryan. As both parties attempted to wrap their candidates in the flag, a flood of star-spangled political advertising helped fuel public support for antidesecration laws.

LEFT AND ABOVE

Pledging allegiance to the flag: New York City, circa 1895; San Francisco, 1942. Children were initially taught to recite the pledge while giving a special salute with the right hand to the forehead and then extended out toward the flag. During World War II, however, many Americans expressed concern that this gesture too closely resembled the Nazi salute. When Congress adopted the U.S. Flag Code in 1942, it replaced the original flag salute with the present custom of placing the right hand over the heart.

National Public School Celebration
COLUMBUS DAY
Oct. 21st.
1492 1892
OFFICIAL BADGE
PATENT AP PLIED FOR

LEFT

Commemorative badge. Millions of children across the United States participated in the National Public School Celebration of Columbus Day in 1892, which introduced the Pledge of Allegiance into American schools.

FROM FAMILY KEEPSAKE
TO NATIONAL TREASURE

A jealous and perhaps selfish love made me guard my treasure with watchful care, lest the trophy of our gallant father should meet with some untoward accident.

—Georgiana Armistead Appleton, February 18, 1873

The first known photograph of the Star-Spangled Banner, taken at the Boston Navy Yard, June 21, 1873, shows the flag already in fragile condition.

Although Francis Scott Key's song was known to nearly every American by the end of the Civil War, the flag that had inspired it remained largely a family keepsake, revered by Baltimoreans but unknown outside of that city until the early 1870s.

Sometime before his death on April 25, 1818, Lieutenant Colonel George Armistead acquired the flag that had been raised over Fort McHenry as the British ships retreated down the river on the morning of September 14, 1814. Exactly how the flag came into his possession remains a mystery. When questioned on the subject in 1873 by naval historian George Preble, Armistead's daughter and namesake, Georgiana Armistead Appleton, said: "I do not know how the flag came into my father's possession—I was not five months old when he died and always accepted the ownership as a fact without question—just as I did any other property. It might have been a usual or granted right for a commander to take a trophy of success." Armistead's granddaughter, Margaret Appleton Baker, said at various times that the flag had been presented to Armistead by the government after the battle. Although this statement has often been repeated in print, historians have never found any documentary evidence to support it. Margaret's brother, Eben Appleton, when pressed

Canvas bag used to store the Star-Spangled Banner when it was shipped to Boston for display in 1873.

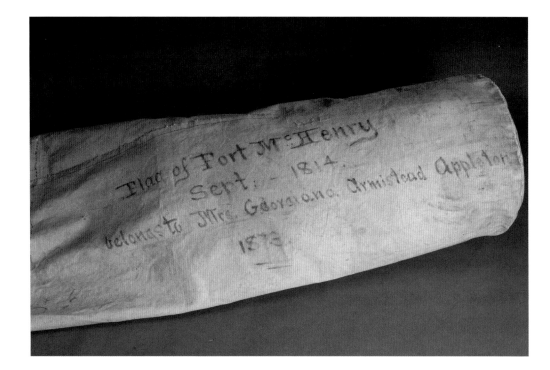

about the matter by a committee of Baltimoreans in 1889, said simply that his grandfather "became the owner of the flag" after the bombardment. Correspondence between Appleton and the Smithsonian that has been preserved in the flag's accession file does not address the issue. However, the Smithsonian's 1907 *Annual Report* described the flag as having been "retained by Colonel George Armistead" after the Battle of Fort McHenry.[1]

In the absence of other clear evidence, it would appear that Armistead decided on his own to keep the Star-Spangled Banner after the battle. He seems to have had strong feelings about the flag because he reportedly wrote his name, followed by the date September 14, 1814, on two of the stripes. Unfortunately, the iron-gall ink Armistead used to write on the flag caused the wool to deteriorate over time, and his signatures are no longer legible. The Star-Spangled Banner remained the private possession of George Armistead's widow and descendants for ninety years. During that time the increasing popularity of Key's anthem and the American public's changing sense of the past transformed the flag from a family keepsake into a national treasure. Its ownership became an increasingly heavy responsibility for Armistead's daughter and for his grandson. It was almost as though the additional layers of significance attached to the flag had literally increased its weight. Eventually the family came to believe that the Star-Spangled Banner belonged in a museum as an artifact of national heritage.

THE BANNER DISPLAYED

When George Armistead died in 1818, the flag he had flown at Fort McHenry passed to his widow, Louisa Hughes Armistead. Louisa took care of the flag for over forty years, occasionally allowing it to be displayed for patriotic events. The flag's first documented public appearance after Lieutenant Colonel Armistead's death occurred on October 8, 1824, when the Marquis de Lafayette visited Baltimore during his commemorative tour of the United States. The return of Lafayette, who as a young French officer had fought heroically alongside George Washington during the American Revolution, triggered an outpouring of patriotic sentiment and memorial tributes to the heroes of the Revolutionary War and the War of 1812, known then as the "Second War of Independence." As Lafayette's party sailed toward Baltimore, soldiers at Fort McHenry fired a salute and hoisted onto the staff "the same 'Star-Spangled Banner' which waved in triumph on that spot during the awful bombardment of 1814." Along with the flag Louisa Armistead also loaned the silver punchbowl service that had been presented to her husband in 1816, and it was used to serve Lafayette and guests during the reception. The Armistead trophies were exhibited at the fort with two relics of George Washington's military service—his tent and camp chest—which had been borrowed for the occasion from Washington's descendants.[2]

In February 1841 the Star-Spangled Banner welcomed another distinguished visitor to the city, president-elect William Henry Harrison. Draped above the speakers' platform, the flag was hailed as "sacred to Baltimore from the battle storm in which it floated in the dark

Portrait and signature of Lieutenant Colonel George Armistead. Engraving from Benson J. Lossing, *The Pictorial Field-Book of the War of 1812*, published by Harper & Brothers, New York, 1868.

Silhouette portrait of Louisa Hughes Armistead. A devoted widow, she used the Star-Spangled Banner to honor the memory of her husband and his fellow defenders of Baltimore.

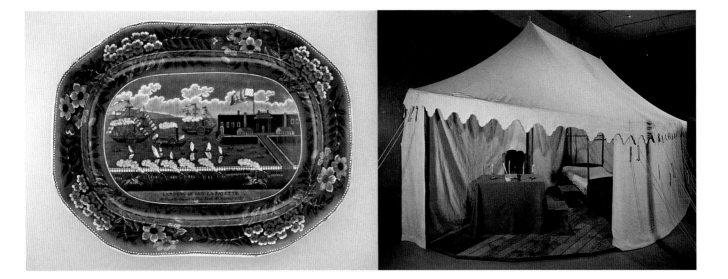

"Landing of Gen. Lafayette at Castle Garden, New York, 16th August 1824." Transfer-printed earthenware platter by James and Ralph Clews, Staffordshire, England, circa 1825–1836. Two months before he visited Fort McHenry, the aging Revolutionary War hero was greeted by patriotic fanfare in New York Harbor.

Tent used by General Washington during the Revolutionary War. His adopted grandson, George Washington Parke Custis, inherited the tent upon Washington's death in 1799 and often made it available for parties and ceremonial gatherings, including the reception of Lafayette at Fort McHenry in 1824. Custis presented the tent to the U.S. government in 1844.

day of her peril." Harrison, himself a War of 1812 hero, had symbolic political ties to the Star-Spangled Banner—during the election campaign the Whig party had used Key's song, as well as images of log cabins flying giant American flags, to associate him with patriotic values. The flag went on display again in May 1844, when the Young Men's Whig National Convention was held in Baltimore. A pamphlet describing the decorations and the processions that wound through the streets beneath them stated: "From the premises of Christopher Hughes Armistead, just above Charles Street, was displayed the identical Star-Spangled Banner which waved over Fort McHenry on the night of its bombardment by the British in 1814; whose waving through 'that perilous night' suggested the thought of that most beautiful of all our National songs—'The Star Spangled Banner.'"[3]

Although these political events linked the Star-Spangled Banner to broader national issues, the flag remained closely tied to local history and traditions throughout this period. Veterans of the Battle of Baltimore, known as the Old Defenders, made the flag a regular feature of Defenders' Day celebrations, held every September 12 to mark the anniversary of the victories at North Point and Fort McHenry. In 1827 and 1828 the Star-Spangled Banner was displayed at ceremonies on Hampstead Hill, where the city had established its main line of defense against the British land invasion during the War of 1812 and which afforded a dramatic view of Fort McHenry across the harbor. A newspaper report of 1828 described how the flag served as the evocative centerpiece for the occasion: "In the centre of the semi-circle a large flag staff had been sunk in the ground, and supported by ropes running to each pavilion, forming the skeleton, as it were, of a roof above the crowd. On the staff we saw the old flag of Fort McHenry . . . amidst the joyous shouts of those who recognized its tattered folds. A holy relic never disgraced, and receiving now the homage of friends, as in 1814 it commanded the respect of foes."[4]

On September 13, 1830, the Star-Spangled Banner made its first appearance at a public museum when it was "politely loaned" by Louisa Armistead to be exhibited at Peale's Museum and Gallery of the Fine Arts. As part of this special Defenders' Day program, the museum presented a "splendid illuminated picture" of the Battle of North Point, measuring 150 square feet, along with a vocal performance of "The Star-Spangled Banner" and the "Marseilles Hymn." The flag was also displayed across the street from Peale's Museum at the Holliday Street theater, where "The Star-Spangled Banner" was first performed in October 1814.[5]

The Old Defenders borrowed the flag once again for a display at North Point on September 12, 1839, the twenty-fifth anniversary of the battle there. According to a newspaper account of the celebration, the Baltimore Independent Blues, a militia company, marched to Louisa Armistead's house early that morning to receive the flag. They escorted it on the steamboat *Rappahannock* to North Point, where it was hung next to the decorated rostrum

Baltimore album quilt (detail) commemorating William Henry Harrison's "Log Cabin Campaign" of 1840.

Georgiana Armistead Appleton, daughter of the defender of Fort McHenry and the guardian of the Star-Spangled Banner from 1861 until her death in 1878. Photograph taken circa 1860.

from which General B. C. Howard gave an address in praise of the "gallant conduct of the brave men who repelled the enemy's fleet from both branches of the Patapsco." After a ceremonial dinner the men returned to the city and marched back to the Armistead house to return the flag.[6]

All this time, the Star-Spangled Banner remained in Baltimore. On only one occasion was it proposed to leave the city: when Francis Scott Key died in January 1843, Louisa Armistead's brother-in-law, Colonel Samuel Moore, offered Key's family the use of the Star-Spangled Banner for his funeral procession. It would appear that the Key family declined, however, as there was no mention of the flag in the newspaper accounts of his funeral.[7]

HANDED DOWN, MOTHER TO DAUGHTER

Before Louisa Armistead died on October 3, 1861, she bequeathed the Star-Spangled Banner that had signaled her husband's triumph at the 1814 Battle of Fort McHenry to her daughter Georgiana Armistead Appleton. The silver service that had been presented to George Armistead by the grateful citizens of Baltimore went to her son, Christopher Hughes Armistead. Although Christopher was disappointed by his mother's decision, his wife, Agnes Gordon Armistead, apparently was glad to be relieved of what she considered to be a burden. A Gordon family story quotes her as having said, "More battles have been fought over that flag than were ever fought under it, and I, for one, am glad to be rid of it!"[8]

In 1873, seeking to explain to naval historian George Henry Preble the flag's location during the Civil War, Georgiana Armistead Appleton also speculated why she and not her brother had inherited the flag: "At the breaking out of the war it [the flag] was in our house but Mr. Appleton immediately broke up housekeeping and our furniture was stored. The flag was then taken for safekeeping to my brother's house in Monument Street, and my mother shortly after went (most unwillingly) with him and his family to Virginia, where she shortly after died, but on his return he was, after some angry words for he thought the flag should have been his, forced to give it up to me and with me it has remained ever since, loved and venerated. . . . Her reasons were that I was called after my father and was the only one of his children born at Fort McHenry. There is a legend that at the time of my birth this banner was raised and the disappointment was great that I was a girl."[9]

The youngest of George and Louisa Armistead's four children, Georgiana was born at Fort McHenry on November 25, 1817. She married William Stuart Appleton on November 27, 1838. A well-connected Bostonian, Appleton was the son of Eben Appleton, one of the founders of the Lowell, Massachusetts, textile mills and the nephew of Nathan Appleton, a Boston textile manufacturer and sometime congressman from Massachusetts. After their marriage the Appletons lived in Baltimore, where he was in the commission and banking business. They had ten children, seven of whom survived to adulthood.

On April 19, 1861, a riot broke out in Baltimore when a mob of Confederate sympathizers confronted troops of the Sixth Massachusetts Volunteer Militia on their way to Washington, D.C. The incident left four soldiers and twelve civilians dead. Federal troops occupied the city for the duration of the war. Engraving from *Frank Leslie's Illustrated Newspaper,* April 30, 1861.

Group of Baltimore merchants, April 21, 1861. Two days after rebel sympathizers attacked federal troops in the city, these men gathered around an American flag to show their loyalty to the Union.

SECESSIONIST SENTIMENTS

Despite her husband's Boston connections, Georgiana Armistead Appleton was a Southern sympathizer in a city that remained part of the Union and was full of Federal troops during the Civil War. In 1861 her son George Armistead Appleton was imprisoned as part of a group of young men who had been trying to go to Virginia to join the Confederate Army. Arrested before he could fight against the nation that his grandfather and namesake had fought to defend, he was held at—of all places—Fort McHenry. Georgiana wrote a letter to her son that unabashedly set forth her Southern sympathies: "I say it is an outrage that you should be left a prisoner. . . . I have no ill or personal feelings for any of my friends who differ in personal opinion from me. I have (thank God) *no drop* of Puritan blood in my body and therefore can be as tolerant as I am and beside that the South can be magnanimous at all times and more particularly now. . . . You know Baltimore the beautiful is empty of men . . . all the 'Rowdies' have enlisted in the Federal Army and all the gentlemen, God save the mark, are in Virginia."[10]

The Appletons probably kept the Star-Spangled Banner in their Baltimore home during the Civil War. Margaret Appleton Baker told a reporter for the *New York Herald* in 1895 that "during the Civil War the flag was sent out of the country, I believe to England, as the city of Baltimore was at that time any but a safe place to remain in." However, no evidence supports her recollection, which would also contradict her mother's 1873 statement to George Preble that the flag stayed in Baltimore.[11]

George Preble's personal collection of Star-Spangled Banner "snippings," which also includes copies of the poem written by Francis Scott Key and the 1873 photograph of the flag. This framed piece hung in Preble's library until his death in 1888; it is now owned by the Peabody Essex Museum in Salem, Massachusetts.

MODIFICATIONS TO THE FLAG

In the antiquarian tradition of relic worship—the veneration of pieces of significant historical objects—Louisa Armistead permitted a number of people to cut small pieces from her flag. Armistead family tradition holds that the first piece was removed to be buried with one of the veterans of the bombardment at the request of a grieving widow. Louisa Armistead's daughter, Georgiana Armistead Appleton, wrote in 1873: "Pieces of the flag have occasionally been given to those who deemed to have a right to such a memento—indeed had we have given all that we had been importuned for little would be left to show." She added that "the star was cut out for some official person" but did not say who that was.[12] One legend sometimes stated in print tells that the star was given to Abraham Lincoln at the beginning of the Civil War, but neither the Lincoln Papers nor any other documentary source reveals any evidence that he received it. Considering the Armisteads' Southern sympathies, the story seems highly unlikely. Other leads pursued by Smithsonian curators over the years have also failed to yield any solution to the mystery of the missing star's whereabouts.

Georgiana Armistead Appleton continued the practice of giving away fragments of the Star-Spangled Banner. By the time it came to the Smithsonian in 1907, the flag had lost more than two hundred square feet of material, much of it presumably to souvenir hunters. About a dozen fragments have been acquired by the Smithsonian over the years; several more have been identified in other museums and private collections.

Pieces of History

Fragments of the Star-Spangled Banner, removed in the 1800s and acquired by the Smithsonian over the past century, represent the desire to own a literal piece of the past. Preserved in various combinations of red, white, and blue, some pieces have been found stuffed in envelopes or tucked into books, long forgotten; others have been framed and carefully labeled, to ensure they would be remembered. Some are loose, with ragged edges; other fragments have been stitched together into a neat row of squares. Some pieces are large, while one is barely the size of a fingertip. In giving away these "snippings," the Armistead family promoted the flag's value as a precious relic and provided individuals with links to its famous history.

During the nineteenth century, relics played a powerful role in how Americans learned about the nation's past. According to one early historian, encounters with objects such as a "glove, a gorget, a lock of hair, [or] a battle map connected by memory with great men or great deeds" could arouse in the viewer "the appropriate emotion of awe and . . . a condition of moral sensitivity and reflection." For

relics invested with national significance, such as those of George Washington and other presidents, this sentimental attachment was not only expected but encouraged as a form of patriotic expression.[1]

Today our national treasures are shared through public museums rather than privately pieced out to souvenir hunters, but the fascination with relics endures. Of the millions of artifacts in the collections of the National Museum of American History, many of the most popular are indeed relics. From the desk on which Thomas Jefferson drafted the Declaration of Independence to the hat President Lincoln wore to Ford's Theatre on the night of his assassination, from the lunch counter where four students launched the Greensboro sit-in to the sequined

ABOVE AND RIGHT
These fragments of the Star-Spangled Banner—pieces of red, white, and blue, removed sometime in the nineteenth century and passed down in the Armistead family—were donated to the Smithsonian in 1988 by the widow of Sumner Appleton Weld, the great-great-grandson of Lieutenant Colonel George Armistead.

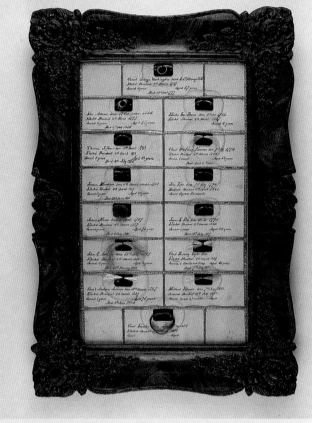

ruby slippers that Judy Garland wore in *The Wizard of Oz*, these objects embody the memories of important people, places, and events. Their value resides not merely in their shape or substance, but in the stories that surround them. As the things that were actually *there*—in the presence of history as it happened—they bring us within one thrilling degree of separation from the heroes and legends of the American past.

ABOVE

A treasured relic of American popular culture, this pair of ruby slippers was worn by Judy Garland as Dorothy in the 1939 movie classic *The Wizard of Oz*.

TOP RIGHT

Nearly fifty years after he drafted the Declaration of Independence, Thomas Jefferson presented this desk to his granddaughter with the following note attached: "Politics, as well as Religion has its superstitions. These, gaining strength with time, may, one day, give imaginary value to this relic, for its association with the birth of the Great Charter of our Independence."

BOTTOM RIGHT

While some Americans collected fragments of the Star-Spangled Banner in the nineteenth century, others pursued different pieces of history. This framed display, acquired by the Smithsonian in 1883, features locks of hair from the first fourteen U.S. presidents.

George Henry Preble, the flag historian who brought the Star-Spangled Banner into the national spotlight during the 1870s.

Red chevron—believed to be the makings of a capital letter *A*—sewn onto the Star-Spangled Banner by Louisa Armistead. A small, embroidered letter *B* appears on the chevron, as does a dark marking that at a distance looks like the letter *M,* but on closer inspection appears to be the number *17.* The significance of these characters is unknown.

Another modification made to the Star-Spangled Banner was the addition of the red chevron onto the third white stripe from the bottom of the flag. Louisa Armistead sewed on this feature, which, according to Georgiana Armistead Appleton, was intended to be the letter *A,* presumably for Armistead. Louisa Armistead may have intended to sew the entire Armistead name onto the stripe, as names of political candidates and even commercial enterprises were commonly printed on

American flags during the nineteenth century. The actual significance of the chevron, however, was known only to Louisa Armistead, who left no record of her intentions—and so this remains another historical mystery.

TOWARD A NATIONAL SYMBOL

The popularity of the song "The Star-Spangled Banner" during the Civil War renewed interest in the flag that was its subject. Indeed, historians began to take an interest in the flag at about the same time that its ownership passed to Georgiana Armistead Appleton in 1861. This

interest led Georgiana to realize that the flag had a national significance that transcended its status as a family treasure.

An Armistead family member informed historian Benson J. Lossing of the flag's existence in 1861, when Lossing was researching his *Pictorial Field-Book of the War of 1812*. Lossing traveled to Baltimore and found the flag at Christopher Hughes Armistead's house. He described his visit in his magazine, *The American Historical Record*: "I called upon Mr. Christopher Hughes Armistead, son of Colonel George Armistead, the commander of Fort McHenry in 1814, who kindly showed me the identical flag of which Key inquired 'O, say, does that star spangled banner yet wave o'er the land of the free and the home of the brave?' Mr. Armistead spread it out on his parlor floor. It was the regular garrison flag faded and worn by exposure to storms and missiles. It had eleven holes in it, made there by the shot of the British during the bombardment of Fort McHenry."[13]

In 1872, Commodore (later Rear Admiral) George Henry Preble brought out the first edition of his massive work *Our Flag: Origin of the Flag of the United States of America*. Preble was unaware, however, of the true history of the actual Star-Spangled Banner. He quoted an unnamed informant as saying that he had been shown the original flag at Fort McHenry in 1852 "rolled up in a piece of dirty muslin and thrown into a corner covered with dust."

After reading that passage in February 1873, Georgiana Armistead Appleton wrote Preble the first of fourteen letters about the flag. In that first letter she outlined the history of the flag's ownership since her father's death in 1818—emphasizing that the flag had not been at Fort McHenry in 1852—as follows: "Had the flag been at Fort McHenry during the rebellion, would not the government have produced it, as the watchword of Union and Liberty? Even then it was mine, and a jealous and perhaps selfish love made me guard my treasure with watchful care, lest this trophy of our gallant father should meet with some untoward accident." Appleton also shared with Preble her change of heart regarding the flag's ownership, stating: "Now I have come to look at the matter in a different light and I think this time honored relic should not remain in private hands, but that it should be in some public place, where our sons and daughters might be taught to look at and love this labarum [standard] of our country."[14]

Preble responded immediately to Georgiana Armistead Appleton, asking if he could have a photograph of the flag, along with an account of the flag's history as she remembered it, to include in the next edition of his book. Having no photograph to send, Georgiana instead shipped the flag by railway express to Preble's office at the Boston Navy Yard in June 1873. Once it arrived, Preble had a canvas backing stitched to the flag so it could be safely unfurled. On June 21 he hung the newly backed flag on the side of a building, where he took the first known photographs of the Star-Spangled Banner. As he wrote to Georgiana Appleton: "I have had the Glorious Old Flag quilted to a sail—and so it was hung out from the 2nd story of one of the buildings at the Navy Yard yesterday afternoon and successfully photographed. I obtained from Col. Jones a couple of Marine privates to stand in full dress and be photographed with it

Centennial Exhibition souvenir fan, 1876.

Decorated with flags and stars in honor of the nation's one hundredth birthday, this patriotic dress was made for Nellie Fletcher, a "Centennial baby" born in Clear Lake, Iowa, in 1876.

to show by comparison its size, and at the same time serve as a guard of honor for the honorable and historic relic." Preble later said that he had intended to have the flag hoisted on the Navy Yard flagstaff and have a twenty-one-gun salute fired to it. He said he soon realized that the "Glorious Old Flag" would be too fragile for that honor.[15]

As the nation's leading authority on the history of the American flag, Commodore Preble quickly became the publicist who placed the Star-Spangled Banner on a national stage. When the flag arrived at the Navy Yard, he wrote an article about it for the *Boston Transcript*. On July 9, 1873, he exhibited the flag at the headquarters of the New England Historic Genealogical Society in Boston along with the flag that had flown on the brig *Enterprise* during its action with the British brig *Boxer* in 1813 and the colors said to have been flown by John Paul Jones's ship, *Bonhomme Richard*. Preble gave a public lecture entitled "Three Historic Flags and Three September Victories," which he later had printed as a pamphlet.

With Georgiana Armistead Appleton's permission, Preble clipped some fragments—he called them "snippings"—from the flag and sent them to friends in the antiquarian world along with copies of the pamphlet and prints, mounted on stiff cardboard, of his photograph of the flag. He also persuaded Georgiana to send photographs of the Rembrandt Peale portrait of her father to some of the recipients.[16]

After Preble's lecture and exhibition the flag was placed in the vault of the New England Historic Genealogical Society. In January 1876 it was moved to the vault of the Historical Society of Pennsylvania, from which it was to have been transported to the Philadelphia Centennial Exhibition for display. But the flag was apparently never displayed in Philadelphia. In

March 1873, before the flag even went to Preble in Boston, Charles B. Norton of the U.S. Centennial Commission, presumably alerted by Preble, wrote to Georgiana Armistead Appleton. He asked if she was interested in exhibiting the flag at the Centennial Exhibition. Nine months later, Georgiana Appleton's Baltimore girlhood friend Alice Taney Campbell Etting also wrote, explaining that she and her husband, Frank Etting, were founding a "National Museum" in Independence Hall in Philadelphia, scheduled to open at the same time as the Centennial Exhibition. She said that she would be presenting a copy of a letter describing her uncle Francis Scott Key's "excursion on which he wrote the 'Star-Spangled Banner'" to the museum and added, "I am very anxious to have the original flag deposited for a while in Independence Hall and write to ask if you will not loan it to us." On Preble's advice, Georgiana Armistead Appleton decided not to lend the flag to the Ettings' National Museum but rather to accept Norton's request to display it at the Philadelphia Centennial Exhibition, as part of the Navy Department exhibit being assembled by Admiral Thornton Jenkins.[17]

Relics of George Washington on exhibit in the U.S. Government Building at the 1876 Centennial Exhibition. The tattered flag used as a backdrop was not the Star-Spangled Banner; although the Fort McHenry flag was shipped to Philadelphia for the fair, it was not displayed.

Admiral Jenkins signed a receipt for the flag, dated January 10, 1876. No evidence exists that he actually displayed the flag, however, even though it is listed in the catalogue of the Navy Department exhibit. Indeed, to the contrary, in July 1876 Preble wrote to Georgiana Appleton: "I visited the Exhibition many times—I found your flag had not been displayed and had a talk with Admiral Jenkins about it who said he had been afraid to put it up fearing it would be mutilated but promised at my suggestion to put it up overhead and out of reach and suitably inscribed—I afterwards wrote him and received in reply a short note saying it would be displayed [with] a printed card in three languages describing it as a relic." The flag did not go on display, however, and the next month Preble wrote Georgiana Appleton to say that he had been "very much annoyed at the non-display." In September she wrote back, asking for Admiral Jenkins's address and stating, "I now intend to have my banner again in my own keeping. Had I known it could not have been worn at the Exhibition I should have loaned it to Mr. Etting."[18]

A year or so before the Centennial Exhibition opened, Georgiana Armistead Appleton evidently had considered making her flag a gift to the nation. In November 1875 her husband's cousin Nathan Appleton Jr. wrote to her saying, "I write now to ask you what are your plans about the Star-Spangled Banner, of which you know we have often talked, that is whether you still think of presenting it to the people of the United States, and allowing me to be the medium of presentation, at some great national fete day as for instance the Fourth of July next and at Philadelphia . . . I would like as I have told you to have the orating part of the programme."[19]

A connection may exist between these conversations with Nathan Appleton and a hand-written inscription on one of the flag's stars, which reads: "This precious relic of my father's fame I . . ." The part of the inscription following the word *I* has been cut out with scissors, and below the hole are the signature "Georgiana Armistead Appleton" and the date July 24, 1876. Georgiana Appleton may have intended to present her flag to the nation during the Philadelphia Centennial Exhibition. She may have then changed her mind, as a result of Admiral Jenkins's "non-display" of the flag.

On June 14, 1877, the one hundredth anniversary of the Flag Act of 1777, Georgiana Armistead Appleton agreed to exhibit her flag in Boston for a national Flag Day celebration. Flags were displayed all over the city, but the celebration focused on the Old South Church, where the Star-Spangled Banner was displayed along with two other historic flags. The mayor of Boston, Frederick O. Prince, served as chairman of the program, and Nathan Appleton Jr. was the principal speaker. Appleton began his Flag Day address with an account of the bombardment of Fort McHenry that drew heavily on Roger B. Taney's letter describing Key's writing of "The Star-Spangled Banner." He summarized the history of flags in general and the development of the U.S. flag in particular. He further quoted several patriotic poems about the American flag, referred to the task of consolidating the Union after the Civil War, and closed by saying he wished every citizen could gaze upon the flag that was there beside the speaker's

Detail of the Star-Spangled Banner, showing Georgiana Armistead Appleton's signature on one of the stars.

rostrum. Specifically Nathan Appleton cited the flag's "simple beauty [to] show mankind, as has never been done before, that social, political, and religious liberty can go hand in hand together."[20]

In the last quarter of the nineteenth century, the Star-Spangled Banner rose substantially in monetary value along with its fame. Despite a severe downturn in her financial situation, Georgiana Armistead Appleton resisted offers to buy the flag. As she wrote to George Preble: "In heavy reverses of fortune when friends have suggested that I might perhaps sell it [the flag] for a high price accepting the overtures that were made for its purchase—I have felt that I would rather beg than part with my treasure."[21]

William Stuart Appleton's business had failed at the beginning of the Civil War, and neither he nor his sons could find employment in Baltimore. Georgiana described her condition as "destitute and suffering" until her husband's uncle Nathan Appleton established a trust fund for her and their children in April 1861. William Stuart Appleton wrote to thank his uncle, saying that he could "only endeavor in the years that remain to me be they few or many to retrieve the property and position that I have lost. My prospects are certainly not very cheering."[22]

Eventually William found employment at the Collector of Customs Office in New York, but as late as 1876, Georgiana was still referring in her correspondence with George Preble to their financial difficulties. She seems to have maintained a kind of philosophical humor amid what were actually rather dire straits. She once wrote Preble about a relative named Mary B. Carter, indicating that she had forgotten whether the "B." stood for "Bowles or Beverly for we are related to both families but not B, the Bankers!"[23]

A HEAVY RESPONSIBILITY

The flag that thirty-three-year-old Eben Appleton inherited on his mother's death on July 25, 1878, had become far more than a family keepsake. The publicity it had received in the 1870s transformed it into a national treasure. Eben Appleton was, in fact, an extremely private man and shunned the inquiries and ultimately the notoriety that his ownership of the Star-Spangled Banner brought him. He locked the flag in a safe-deposit vault in downtown Manhattan and refused to disclose its location. Appleton had no sooner locked up the flag than he received the first of what he later remembered to be at least twenty requests to lend his relic to a civic celebration. This first request came from his native city, Baltimore, where the City Council was planning to lay the cornerstone to the Eutaw Street monument to George Armistead as part of the city's five-day sesquicentennial celebration in October 1880. In view of the honor being paid to his grandfather, Appleton agreed to bring the flag to Baltimore.[24]

On October 13, 1880, the Star-Spangled Banner was carried through the streets of Baltimore as part of a military parade led by two artillery batteries and a company of infantry from Fort McHenry. The fort's twenty-two-piece band and a contingent of sailors and marines from the USS *Kearsage* and the USS *Vandalia* followed. A decorated carriage drove behind

them, carrying nine of the remaining Old Defenders—men in their eighties and nineties by this time, dressed in black dress suits and top hats. One of these surviving heroes, Henry Lightner, carried a battered kettledrum in his arms. The carriage was escorted by a color guard of Grand Army of the Republic veterans. Behind, in another carriage, came the Star-Spangled Banner, folded in the lap of William W. Carter, a local historian and proponent of the Armistead monument. Militia companies and volunteer firemen from all over Maryland, their horse-drawn engines decked with flowers, brought up the rear. A newspaper account of the parade indicated that "as the tattered old relic was seen by the crowds, their enthusiasm was unbounded."[25]

This parade was the last time that the Star-Spangled Banner was seen in Baltimore. But as the flag was being packed for shipment back to New York, Appleton invited Carter to snip three fragments—one red, one white, and one blue—from the sixty-seven-year-old flag.[26] Carter framed the pieces and presented them to the Maryland Historical Society. In 1926 the society donated the objects to the Smithsonian Institution.

Eben Appleton took quite seriously his responsibility as a trustee of a national treasure. In 1889 he declined to lend the flag to a committee of Baltimoreans who were planning a five-day celebration of the seventy-fifth anniversary of the bombardment. Appleton felt that the occasion, which included an agricultural and industrial arts fair, lacked the decorum

Eben Appleton (1845–1925), Lieutenant Colonel George Armistead's grandson and the last private owner of the Star-Spangled Banner.

The Old Defenders at Druid Hill Park, Baltimore, October 1880.

Ceremonial arch honoring
Francis Scott Key and "The Star-
Spangled Banner," erected for
Baltimore's sesquicentennial
celebration, October 1880.

befitting the flag. There followed a series of misunderstandings not only about the nature of the celebration but also about the way in which the flag would be displayed. A rift developed between Appleton and Francis P. Stevens, the committee chairman. Stevens announced to the Baltimore press that the flag had always been government property, that it did not legally belong to Appleton, and that he intended to see the secretary of war and force Appleton to give it up.

A committee headed by Stevens did call on the acting secretary of war, General Robert Macfeely, who sent a tactful letter to Appleton that did not raise the matter of ownership but simply suggested that Appleton "should be pleased to comply with the reasonable request of the citizens of Baltimore." Appleton wrote a polite reply, saying that to lend the flag under the circumstances would be inconsistent with his duty to preserve the flag. He cited the flag's poor condition and depredations of relic hunters and also expressed the opinion that the Baltimore celebration was not "an occasion of great national interest."[27]

Privately Eben Appleton was enraged at the suggestion that the flag was not legally his and at the action of the committee in approaching General Macfeely. A reporter for the *Baltimore American* described an interview in Appleton's New York home during which the flag's keeper gestured toward a picture of his grandfather and said, "Does that look like the face of a man who would claim property not his own?"[28] To add insult to injury, the committee visited Appleton's home at 71 East 54th Street to renew their plea. Appleton responded emphatically that the flag would not be made available to them. At a second meeting the next day at the Astor House hotel, Appleton remained adamant and refused to disclose the location of the flag, which was still in its safe-deposit vault.[29]

Meanwhile, a group of Baltimore ladies who were descendants of the Old Defenders announced that in view of Appleton's refusal to send the flag to Baltimore, they intended to create a full-size replica of it for use at the celebration. On September 8, 1889, Miss Adah Schley presented the replica—along with some unkind remarks about Appleton—to the mayor of Baltimore. This incident and the publicity it received in the Baltimore and New York newspapers upset Appleton tremendously. According to his sister, Georgiana Appleton Hunter, Eben Appleton refused for the next eighteen years to discuss the flag or to disclose his address, "having been much annoyed on account of his heirloom all his life."[30]

When he entered his early sixties, Eben Appleton began to address his concerns about the flag's future. He had no male heirs. Looking beyond his family, he decided to seek a public home for the Star-Spangled Banner.

THE STAR-SPANGLED BANNER
COMES TO THE SMITHSONIAN

It has always been my intention to present the flag during my lifetime to that institution in the country where it could be conveniently seen by the public, and where it would be well cared for, and the advantages and appropriateness of the National Museum are so obvious, as to render the consideration of any other place unnecessary.

—Eben Appleton, December 12, 1912

Eben Appleton lent the Star-Spangled Banner to the Smithsonian Institution in 1907. In 1912 he converted the loan to a gift. On January 10, 1914, he wrote to Smithsonian Secretary Charles Walcott, saying, "I . . . congratulate myself daily upon it being in such competent hands, and anything you may deem best to be done for its preservation and display will always have my hearty approval."[1]

With the benefit of historical perspective, it appears inevitable that the Star-Spangled Banner would eventually take its rightful place as one of the nation's most treasured symbols in the world's largest museum complex. But despite the nation's rising enthusiasm for national history and patriotic symbols in the years following the Civil War, there was no guarantee that the Smithsonian Institution, established in 1846 as an organization for scientific research, was either the rightful or logical repository for such a relic.

By the turn of the twentieth century, however, the Smithsonian had evolved. Although it remained an academically minded institution committed to the increase of knowledge about the natural world, it had also widened its focus and inquisitive prowess. Beginning in the 1870s, efforts to create a national museum that displayed and documented America's historical past

Visitors to the United States
National Museum, circa 1900.

The relics of George Washington on exhibit in the United States National Museum, 1891.

transformed the Smithsonian into a truly national center for exploration and education. It was to this "new" Smithsonian that the Appleton family would finally entrust their most sacred family keepsake.

ESTABLISHING THE UNITED STATES NATIONAL MUSEUM

In leaving his estate to the American people, British scientist James Smithson (1765–1829) challenged the U.S. government to create an institution dedicated to the increase and diffusion of knowledge, but he did not provide a specific plan, vision, or direction detailing his expectations of what form the new institution should take. The announcement of Smithson's gift in 1835 touched off a national debate as to whether the institution should be a library, university, astronomical observatory, scientific research institute, or even a national museum. The Smithsonian's first secretary, noted physicist Joseph Henry, used his influence to shape the new Smithsonian in the mold of traditional scientific research institutes. Henry strived to expand the state of scientific knowledge in the United States and advance the nation's reputation as a scientific power.

Objects that spoke about the nation's history and the accomplishments of its leaders were regarded as curious relics and not germane to the Smithsonian's more "scholarly" pursuits. Initially, such collections were housed in the Patent Office Building (the future home of the Smithsonian American Art Museum and the Smithsonian's National Portrait Gallery). The Patent Office Building displayed the models submitted by inventors, but one could also find James Smithson's mineralogical cabinet, George Washington's field kit, and a printing press once used by Benjamin Franklin there. Nearby, portraits and statues, as well as other industrial artifacts and relics that had been owned and used by America's military leaders, were poised next to the ethnological collections brought to Washington, D.C., from around the world by the United States Exploring Expeditions. Under the auspices and care of the National Institute for the Promotion of Science, this eclectic collection of items formed a venerable "Cabinet of Curiosities" that represented the holdings of the federal government. But this random assortment of items could hardly be regarded as the proud display of a truly national museum.

But just as the American people became much more interested in and appreciative of their own history after the Civil War, the Smithsonian expanded its focus and efforts to record and document the American past. The 1876 Centennial Exhibition at Philadelphia, as did previous World's Fairs, showcased the nation's industrial, mechanical, and scientific achievements. But as a celebration of one hundred years of American independence, the exposition also looked back at the past through the display of cultural objects and notable relics. Henry's assistant, Spencer Fullerton Baird, was appointed to organize the Smithsonian and other U.S. government exhibits in Philadelphia. The Smithsonian exhibit was overwhelmingly popular and considered to be the most successful of the entire exposition.

Unlike Henry, Baird strongly desired to create a true national museum in Washington and capitalized on the success of the Philadelphia exhibition to further his dream. Baird convinced the other exhibitors at the fair to donate their displays and specimens to the Smithsonian, and he returned to Washington with sixty railroad cars filled with objects. This far exceeded the storage and exhibit capacity at the Smithsonian's sole building, affectionately known as the Castle, and the items were instead stored in the Armory Building. When Secretary Henry died on May 13, 1878, Baird succeeded him as secretary. He lost no time in going to Congress seeking support for his plan, and on March 3, 1879, $250,000 was appropriated for a new national museum building. In 1881, Baird and his colleagues formally established the United States National Museum (in what is now known as the Arts and Industries Building) as a showcase for the nation's history, resources, and treasures.

Among the tremendous Smithsonian collections of scientific specimens, historical artifacts began to take their place in the national collections. Although a small number of objects from the U.S. Patent Office came to the Smithsonian in 1858, it was not until the 1880s that many of the more significant objects from the "Cabinet of Curiosities"—such as George Washington's sword and Benjamin Franklin's walking stick—were transferred to the Smithsonian. The Institution's new emphasis on these "personal relics of representative men" and the "memorials of events or places of historical importance" reflected its expanding efforts to understand and illustrate the history of human culture and "become the most comprehensive and instructive educational exhibit in the world."[2]

A GIFT TO THE NATION

In 1907, when Eben Appleton decided to unburden himself of his treasure, he first corresponded with both the governor of Maryland and the mayor of Baltimore about donating the flag to the state or the city. Soon after, Appleton was approached by a history-minded cousin, John B. Baylor, employed by the U.S. Coast and Geodetic Survey and an acquaintance of Smithsonian Secretary Walcott. Baylor wrote to Walcott, describing his kinship to Appleton and asking Walcott to "second my efforts to convince Mr. Appleton to either lend or give his flag to the National Museum." "If you handle him in a tactful manner," Baylor said, "I believe he will do this." Baylor enclosed a letter he had received from Appleton saying that the National Museum at the Smithsonian appealed to him more than any other option for placing the flag. Walcott replied immediately to Baylor, saying, "The addition of this notable object to the historical collections of the National Museum would be very deeply appreciated," and that "it would be acceptable either as a loan or a gift, and would be given a conspicuous position such as it deserves."

Baylor passed along Secretary Walcott's letter to Appleton, who then wrote to Walcott. Appleton stated that he had often thought it would be a good idea to exhibit the flag "in one of the public buildings in Washington" and asked for more information about the Institution and its policies. By June 30, Appleton had decided to lend the flag to the Smithsonian. He asked only to be reassured that the Smithsonian would not in turn lend the flag to any third party without his consent. Packed in the wooden crate that Commodore George Preble had made for it in 1876, the flag was shipped from New York by Adams Express on July 5, 1907, and arrived at the Smithsonian the next day. Secretary Walcott was out of town when the banner came, but Assistant Secretary Richard Rathbun had it hung on the exterior wall of the Castle and photographed. The flag was then placed in a case in the Arts and Industries Building's Hall of History, next to cases holding military artifacts that had belonged to George Washington and Ulysses S. Grant. Rathbun wrote Appleton that "[the Star-Spangled Banner's] presence in the museum has caused a wave of patriotism, which it is very good to see." The exceptionally large flag had to be folded a number of times to fit into the case.[3]

In 1912, Eben Appleton decided to convert the loan to a gift. The only condition that he attached at that time was that the Smithsonian display an exhibit label near the flag that identified it as the flag that was defended by Lieutenant Colonel George Armistead and his men and that inspired Francis Scott Key to write the verses of "The Star-Spangled Banner." A year later Appleton added the condition that the flag not leave the Smithsonian under any circumstance. The event that precipitated this stipulation was an attempt by the National Star-Spangled Banner Centennial Commission in Baltimore to have the flag brought to Baltimore for their September 1914 celebration. The Baltimore commission's request began in December 1913, when Arthur A. Bibbins, chair of the Centennial Commission, called on Secretary Walcott and proposed that the Smithsonian restore the flag and then lend it to the centennial celebration. Walcott consulted with Assistant Secretary Rathbun, who told him

The Star-Spangled Banner was displayed for a photograph on the Smithsonian Institution Building (the Castle) shortly after it arrived at the Smithsonian in 1907.

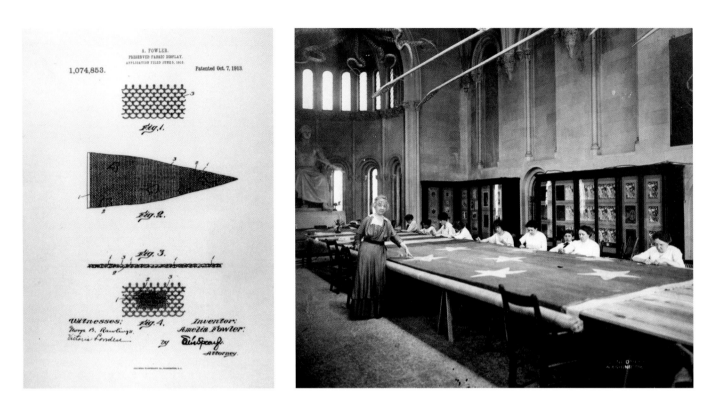

Patent issued to Amelia Fowler
on October 7, 1913, for "new
and useful improvements in
preserved fabric display."

Amelia Fowler and her team
sew the new linen support to
the Star-Spangled Banner in
the Smithsonian Institution
Building, 1914.

that the flag could never be restored to a condition that would permit it to travel. He said specifically: "If taken away it would most likely fall to pieces." Walcott conveyed this observation to Bibbins in a polite letter, in which he also stated that the Smithsonian had recently refused to lend the flag to the Toledo Museum of Art and would have to decline to lend it to Baltimore as well.

In the meantime, Bibbins had written directly to Eben Appleton, asking him to use his influence with Secretary Walcott to have the Smithsonian transfer the flag's ownership to the City of Baltimore, to be permanently displayed in a memorial hall to be built at Fort McHenry. Horrified, Appleton fired off a letter to Walcott, asking what he might do to prevent the Smithsonian from ever lending or donating the flag. Appleton said he had given the flag to the Smithsonian "with practically no condition attached to the gift, because I could not conceive of the authorities donating to any one or any place anything which had been given to them." Walcott reassured him that, if he so desired, the flag would never leave the museum, even temporarily. He asked Appleton for a letter specifically stating that condition. Appleton wrote back on January 10, 1914, saying, "I gave the flag to the National Museum with the firm and settled intention of having it remain there forever and regarded the acceptance of the gift by the Authorities of the Museum as an evidence of their willingness to comply with this condition, and I could not for one moment consent to its transfer to any other place, even temporarily."[4]

In spite of this unequivocal statement, Bibbins and the National Star-Spangled Banner Centennial Commission pursued their request for the loan of the flag with the secretary of war, the House Committee on Military Affairs, and Eben Appleton's own daughter, Mrs. William E. Morton. So certain was the commission of its success that it printed a statement in the program for the Star-Spangled Banner Centennial Celebration that the original Star-Spangled Banner was to be carried in a Baltimore parade on September 12, 1914. On August 31, 1914, Appleton proclaimed to Walcott: "Therefore, let us all stand firm at *this time* and at *all* times, and under *all* circumstance, and let any American citizen who visits the museum with the expectation of seeing the flag be sure of finding it in its accustomed place." He described the pressure that was being brought upon him and his determination not to give in to it.[5]

"JUST FADING AWAY"

From the day that the flag arrived at the Smithsonian Institution Building on the National Mall, Smithsonian officials recognized that it was in delicate condition. As early as 1873, Georgiana Armistead Appleton had described the flag as "just fading away, being among our earthly treasures where moth and rust must corrupt."[6] In 1907, Assistant Secretary Rathbun wrote to Eben Appleton that the flag's canvas backing was too heavy for it and that he might suggest a new backing. Soon after he met with Secretary Walcott in December 1913, Arthur Bibbins mentioned to Walcott that the historical flag collection at the U.S. Naval Academy in Annapolis had been preserved by Amelia Fowler of Boston. Bibbins suggested that Fowler might do the same for the Star-Spangled Banner.

Early in February 1914, Theodore Belote, a Smithsonian assistant curator of history, was dispatched to Annapolis to look at the Naval Academy flags. He enthusiastically reported back his findings and explained Fowler's preservation method, which involved stitching each flag to a linen backing with a net stitch. Belote recommended that the Smithsonian retain Fowler to treat the Star-Spangled Banner in the same way so that "it would then be feasible to suspend it lengthwise on the west wall of the North Hall with the Union in the upper left corner."[7] On March 25, 1914, Rathbun wrote to Fowler asking for her terms for sewing a new backing to the Star-Spangled Banner. Just more than a hundred years after Mary Pickersgill (and her family) made the flag in Baltimore, the first steps to preserve it were taken.[8]

Amelia Bold Fowler was a teacher of embroidery who became involved in flag preservation in 1900, when she advised the State of Massachusetts on the preservation of the Civil War flags displayed at the State House in Boston. In 1912 she and a team of forty needlewomen she had trained were retained by the U.S. Naval Academy to preserve a collection of 172 historical flags. From that work she developed a method of preservation that she patented in 1913. This method involved laying a flag—or in some cases the remaining pieces of a flag—out on a piece of unbleached Irish or Belgian linen that was cut to the size of the flag. The flag was then ironed flat with an electric iron and stitched to the linen backing with an

Fowler and her team worked through the hot and humid summer of 1914 in an un-air-conditioned building to complete the preservation effort.

interlocking network of stitches that formed a mesh of thread over the face of the flag, holding it to the backing with about twelve stitches per square inch. Before being stitched into place, the thread was carefully dyed to match the portion of the flag that it would cover so that the resulting mesh would blend in with the flag.[9]

Fowler agreed to do the work on the Star-Spangled Banner under a government contract for a total fee of $1,243, which included $243 for materials, $500 to pay a team of ten needle-women, and a $500 fee for herself. Fowler's team laid out the flag on a set of makeshift tables in the room in the Castle then known as the chapel (now the Commons), where American sculptor Horatio Greenough's seated statue of George Washington was displayed. Fowler and her team worked for eight weeks between mid-May and mid-July 1914. The needle-women removed the canvas backing that Commodore Preble's sailors had sewn on in 1873 and sewed on a new linen backing using approximately 1,700,000 stitches. They sewed the linen backing to the same side of the flag that the canvas backing had been on. This meant that when the flag was displayed in a horizontal position, the union was on the viewer's right, rather than on the left as the Flag Code passed by the National Flag Conference in 1923 would require. After this deviation was repeatedly pointed out by visitors, the Smithsonian eventually added a label explaining that the flag was backed and mounted before the passage of the Flag Code.

Shortly following the completion of the conservation treatment, Fowler recorded her thoughts, observations, and feelings about the Star-Spangled Banner, declaring it to be "the most impressive flag in the possession of the Nation." She wrote eloquently about what she considered to be the flag's importance as an enduring symbol of perseverance and freedom, stating that "what the flag stood for in the day of trial it stands for still, and always will."[10]

The newly backed flag was mounted in a horizontal position in a specially constructed case on the west wall of the North Hall of the Arts and Industries Building, just to the right of the main entrance. Although the case was nearly seventeen feet high and thirty-five feet long, it was not tall enough for the entire flag to be displayed, and so the lower half was folded up in the bottom of the case. A layer of naphthalene flakes in the bottom of the case protected its contents from insect damage. Only the blue union and its stars and the top half of the stripes were visible to visitors.[11] In 1921, George Armistead's great-grandson, Alexander

The Star-Spangled Banner in its case at the Smithsonian Institution's Arts and Industries Building, 1949.

111

Hidden Treasure

One of the few conditions Eben Appleton insisted on when he converted his loan of the Star-Spangled Banner into a permanent gift to the Smithsonian in 1912 was that the flag never leave the Institution under any circumstances. Appleton directed Smithsonian Secretary Charles D. Walcott to ensure that any "citizen who visits the museum with the expectation of seeing the flag be sure of finding it in its accustomed place."[1] For its part, the Smithsonian has lived up to its pledge and the Star-Spangled Banner has never left the confines of the Institution—with one notable exception.

After German bombers launched their bombing "blitz" on London in September 1940, destroying both military and civilian targets, including government repositories and museums, American leaders took action to prevent a similar tragedy in Washington, D.C. In March 1941, President Franklin D. Roosevelt formally established the Committee on Conservation of Cultural Resources, comprised of the leaders of America's foremost cultural institutions, to consider the best means of saving the nation's treasures from attack.

According to the Institution's 1942 *Annual Report,* preparing for a possible attack on the National Mall consumed the energies and expertise of Smithsonian staff. Air-raid and blackout drills were conducted, and boxes of sand (to be used in case of fire) were placed in attics throughout the Institution. In addition, curators and historians began the near-impossible task of surveying the collections and selecting items of scientific importance, artistic wonder, and irreplaceable historical significance for evacuation out of the city.

In 1942, just after the country had entered the war the previous December, the Smithsonian secretly transported sixty tons of its most valued and prized collections to an eighty-six-thousand-square-foot warehouse facility owned by the National Park Service in Shenandoah National Park in the Blue Ridge Mountains near Luray, Virginia. The nation's most significant historical objects were hidden away in nondescript and isolated warehouses alongside specimens of the natural world and paintings crafted by masters of art—not to be seen or admired by the public for two long years. George Washington's uniform, sword, and camp chest made the journey, accompanied by Benjamin Franklin's walking stick, the writing desk on which Thomas Jefferson drafted the Declaration of Independence, gowns worn by America's First Ladies, and Abraham Lincoln's plaster death mask. Other significant collections sent to safety included the National Philatelic Collection, a collection of the nation's patent models, and a small arsenal of weapons—handguns, rifles, and swords. Along with a fine array of china, furniture, and scientific apparatus, the entire American Flag Collection was sent away—including the extraordinary step of moving the Star-Spangled Banner. The flag that had inspired the national anthem was folded and placed in a fifteen-foot-long, specially constructed crate and moved out of the National Museum to the safety of the mountains.[2]

This fantastic collection of artifacts was placed under twenty-four-hour guard. By late 1944 it was apparent that the nation was safe from bombing attacks, and the Smithsonian and the National Park Service returned America's treasures to their proper homes. And once again, the Star-Spangled Banner returned to its place in the National Museum, where it would stand as an inspiration to countless visitors, just as Eben Appleton had intended.

During World War II sixty tons of the Smithsonian's most significant treasures were temporarily transferred to Shenandoah National Park near Luray, Virginia, for safekeeping.

Gordon, presented the Smithsonian with the silver service that the citizens of Baltimore had bestowed on Armistead in 1816. The Smithsonian placed the set in a case next to the flag.

For nearly fifty years the Arts and Industries Building served as the home of the Star-Spangled Banner and other objects telling stories about America's past.[12] During that time the Smithsonian did its best to care for the flag and fulfill Eben Appleton's wishes that it be kept on permanent display for the American people. The 1914 conservation treatment made it possible to hang the fragile banner so visitors could get a sense of its scale, while the glass case afforded a close-up view of the tattered stripes and stars. With the exception of two years during World War II, when it was removed from Washington, D.C., along with other national treasures for safekeeping in case of enemy attack, the Star-Spangled Banner remained a popular and constant presence on the National Mall. But as the national collections continued to expand, the Smithsonian contemplated new and more effective ways to showcase its historical treasures.

THE NATION'S ATTIC?

By the beginning of the twentieth century, the Smithsonian had emerged as a national center for exploration and public education. The collection and display of scientific wonders and historical relics made it the proper and logical repository for the Star-Spangled Banner, whose reputation as a national symbol of resilience and perseverance had grown significantly. But the fierce pace of collecting objects outran the capacity of the National Museum to display them effectively and store them properly.

The opening of the National Museum of Natural History in 1911 meant new space to house the enormous scientific and ethnographic holdings of the Institution and that in turn meant more space for the documentation of America's historical legacy in the Arts and Industries Building. But the relief was temporary, and Smithsonian curators once again lamented the lack of suitable exhibition and storage space for the national collections. The Arts and Industries Building became crammed with the nation's most prized objects that, for lack of space, were packed in rows of exhibit cases, mounted on walls, or hung from the rafters. It became difficult to present meaningful information to the visitor beyond a simple identification label, and there was no cohesive strategy governing the organization of the exhibits. The display of the Star-Spangled Banner was no exception. The flag that had inspired the national anthem remained folded and displayed in half, hidden from view by other displays and other objects. Although visitorship to the Arts and Industries Building in the 1950s surpassed more than two million people a year, critics wondered if the Smithsonian was providing a significant and engaging educational experience to those who visited its halls.

Smithsonian Secretary Leonard Carmichael was also concerned. "From my windows overlooking the Mall," he wrote in the 1950s, "I see a constant stream of visitors entering our Arts & Industries building." Although he was appreciative of the visitors' enthusiasm, Carmichael feared that the idiosyncratic exhibitions and "the press of objects" would overwhelm

them. He concluded that the "crowded exhibits" presented a "confused impression of our history and technology."[13] Silvio A. Bedini, a future deputy director of the Museum of History and Technology, described the cacophonous display in the National Museum as the genesis of the Smithsonian's reputation as the "nation's attic."[14]

Smithsonian leaders feared that the Institution would be forced to refuse donations of new "historic" and "irreplaceable" gifts to the collections for lack of space to care for and exhibit them.[15] In response, Carmichael, along with Frank A. Taylor, then serving as the director of the Department of Engineering and Industries for the National Museum, called for an entirely new museum devoted to the study of American history, technology, culture, and manufacturing, in which the proper display of the national collections would serve to document the "material evidence of our national growth and achievement." Instead of a nearly random display of disparate objects, the enlarged space of the new museum would allow the Smithsonian to present a cohesive story of the nation's development and achievements using authentic historical objects.[16] The new Museum of History and Technology would enable the Smithsonian to fulfill its obligation to disseminate knowledge and meet the educational needs of the public.[17]

By the 1930s the Arts and Industries Building had become overwhelmed with exhibits. In the North Hall the *Spirit of St. Louis* hung over rows and rows of cases packed with objects, including the Star-Spangled Banner, which was grouped with other military relics.

...we here highly resolve that these de[ad]
shall not have died in vain...

REMEMBER DEC. 7th!

BELOW
"America First" pennant, Crookston, Minnesota. The America First Committee, an isolationist group that opposed U.S. intervention in World War II, was founded in 1940. It attracted a large following, especially in the Midwest, and its leaders included aviator Charles Lindbergh. Shortly after the attack on Pearl Harbor in December 1941, the committee dissolved.

RIGHT
Office of War Information poster. Artist Allen Saalburg's powerful image of the tattered flag flying at half-staff evoked the nation's grief and outrage after the Japanese attack on Pearl Harbor and urged Americans to channel those emotions into action. The quotation at the top, from Abraham Lincoln's Gettysburg Address, recalled an earlier time when Americans also rallied around the flag.

MEANINGS AND MEMORIES   # THE FLAG

During World War II the American flag emerged once again to rally and inspire the nation in a time of crisis. On both the battlefield and the home front, the flag symbolized the values and freedoms the nation was fighting for, and it called on citizens to support those ideals through service and sacrifice. By the end of the war the flag had become the emblem of a superpower with a mission to promote democracy around the world.

Before the nation entered the war, however, the flag was more commonly raised to oppose American involvement in international conflicts. Isolationist sentiments had dominated U.S. foreign policy in the years following World War I, and when war broke out in Europe again in 1939, many Americans believed the country should remain neutral. Yet such calls to put America "first" quickly evaporated after the Japanese attack on the U.S. military base at Pearl Harbor, Hawaii, on December 7, 1941. As had happened at Fort McHenry in 1814 and Fort Sumter in 1861, the image of the Star-Spangled Banner under attack inspired a wave of patriotism and unity and renewed popular reverence for the flag.

While the military strength of the U.S. armed forces transformed the American flag into an icon of freedom and power abroad, the federal government also depended on the flag to mobilize and sustain support for the war at home. Posters, billboards, magazines, and movies waved the Star-Spangled

BELOW

Milk-bottle collar. As the nation's industries shifted to war production, many consumer items became scarce commodities. Rationing and recycling became a patriotic duty, a way for every American to pitch in and support the war effort.

RIGHT

Children in Chicago collecting scrap for the war effort. Photograph by Jack Delano, 1942.

Each Milk Bottle lost or destroyed means precious material and man-hours wasted. and speeding empty bottles back to the dairy. Speed Victory by

★ ★ Milk consumers in every State are urged to help lengthen the life of MILK BOTTLES by using them carefully and returning them promptly when empty.

RETURN WHEN EMPTY
and you'll help
WIN THE WAR

IN WORLD WAR II

Banner to urge Americans to buy bonds, produce for victory, ration and recycle, and make other personal sacrifices for the greater good. Such appeals linked the flag not only to a sense of loyalty but also to shared cultural values, casting the war as a struggle to defend the "American way of life" against the forces of totalitarianism.

Yet this vision of America as a defender of democracy was challenged by the realities of racism and inequality. The same flag that liberated Nazi camps in Europe flew over internment camps in the western United States, where Japanese Americans were imprisoned by executive order from 1942 until the war's end. The American GIs who fought together under the flag served in racially segregated units. During the war African Americans and other minority groups used the Star-Spangled Banner not only to display their patriotism, but to call attention to these injustices and claim their equal rights as U.S. citizens.

The artifacts and images on these pages reflect how Americans used the flag during World War II to express ideas about both what it meant to be American in a time of war and what was worth fighting for.

WE CAN...
WE WILL..
WE MUST!
..Franklin D. Roosevelt

BUY U.S. **WAR SAVINGS BONDS** & **STAMPS** NOW

ABOVE

U.S. Treasury Department poster.
Designed by artist Carl Paulson
in 1941 under the direction of the
Outdoor Advertising Association
of America, Inc., this image of
the American flag appeared
on thousands of billboards
nationwide in the spring of 1942.
Its eye-catching design and
straightforward message linked
the flag to wartime ideals of
patriotism, service, and sacrifice.

ABOVE

Manzanar barracks sign. On
February 19, 1942, President
Franklin Roosevelt signed Executive Order 9066, authorizing the
internment of people of Japanese
descent in the interest of national
security. Almost 120,000 men,
women, and children—the
majority of them U.S. citizens—
were forced from their homes
into detention camps.

ABOVE

**War Relocation Authority Center,
Manzanar, California.** Photograph
by Dorothea Lange, 1942.

OPPOSITE PAGE

Ella Watson, August 1942. While
working for the Farm Security
Administration in Washington,
D.C., African American photographer Gordon Parks was shocked
and disillusioned by the racial
prejudice he encountered in the
nation's capital. He used the flag
ironically to express these feelings
in his famous portrait of Watson,
who worked as a cleaning woman
in a government office building.

TOP LEFT

Souvenir pillow top. Mementos given by servicemen to loved ones often used the flag to symbolize and reinforce the emotional bonds of home, family, and nation. The Tennessee Maneuvers were battlefield training exercises conducted from 1941 until 1944.

TOP MIDDLE

Jacket patch. Escape flags, or blood chits, served as survival tools for downed U.S. fliers who needed to communicate with foreign allies in order to return to safety. This patch was worn by Robert B. Frank, who served in the China-Burma-India theater with the U.S. Army Air Forces. It features the U.S. and Chinese national flags, along with a message in Chinese that identifies the bearer as an American and asks for help and protection.

TOP RIGHT AND RIGHT

GI's handmade flag. Joseph E. Fennimore (kneeling, second from left) was a scout with the Eighth Regiment of the Fourth Infantry Division, which spearheaded the Allied invasion of Germany in early 1945. When he discovered his company command post had no American flag to fly, Fennimore created one using a captured Nazi flag, a blue dress uniform, and some salvaged red fabric. His squad proudly posed with the flag on May 7, 1945, the day Germany surrendered unconditionally to the Allies.

Raising the flag at Iwo Jima.
On this tiny island 650 miles
from Tokyo, U.S. Marines fought
entrenched Japanese forces in one
of the bloodiest battles of the war
and secured a critical foothold for
the Allied air campaign against
mainland Japan. On February 23,
1945, Associated Press

photographer Joe Rosenthal
snapped a picture as five marines
and a navy hospital corpsman
raised a flag to signal the capture
of Mount Suribachi. The image
became an iconic expression of
American military valor and rallied
the nation during the final months
of World War II.

CENTERPIECE OF
A NEW MUSEUM

A growing country needs a growing national museum able at all times to house, record, and display before the world the historic material evidence of our national growth and achievement.

—Smithsonian Secretary Leonard Carmichael, early 1950s

Architect's drawing of the proposed Flag Hall at the Museum of History and Technology, circa 1960.

In 1964 the Star-Spangled Banner became the dramatic centerpiece of the Smithsonian's newest museum on the National Mall. The Museum of History and Technology, later renamed the National Museum of American History, established a permanent home for the Smithsonian's collection of national historical treasures, from Thomas Jefferson's desk and Abraham Lincoln's hat to First Ladies' gowns and Thomas Edison's lightbulb. Of all the artifacts featured in the new building, the most prominent and celebrated was the flag that had inspired the national anthem.

Impressively displayed in the Museum's Flag Hall, suspended on a vertical backdrop that filled in the missing stripes and star, the Star-Spangled Banner was transformed from a tattered relic into a patriotic icon—an inspiring emblem, in the words of Smithsonian officials, of "our heritage of freedom."[1] From this position of honor the banner looked down on inaugural balls, presidential speeches, and other public ceremonies and was admired by millions of Americans. As both artifact and symbol, it assumed a central role in the story of America told within the walls of the new Museum.

A NEW PLAN FOR A NEW MUSEUM

For decades the growth of the national collections had threatened to overwhelm the exhibits in the Arts and Industries Building. In the 1950s Smithsonian officials, led by Secretary Leonard Carmichael and Curator Frank Taylor, began to develop and promote a plan for a new museum focusing on American history and culture. Carmichael and Taylor found support for their vision in the United States Congress, which after World War II sought a reaffirmation of patriotism and nationalism in the face of the Soviet Union's challenge to American supremacy and Cold War threats. The creation of a Museum of History and Technology would provide a dynamic stage to present the cultural, political, and technological achievements of the United States and to educate American citizens about the vital roles of freedom, individualism, industry, and courage in U.S. society. Or as Remington Kellogg, then serving as the director of the United States National Museum, observed about the new museum: "It is equally needed for the opportunity it gives to awaken in citizen and foreigner alike a clear understanding of the inspiring story of the United States—its origins, struggles, development, traditions, strength. . . . Its exhibits are planned to instill in each citizen a deepened faith in his country's destiny as a champion of individual dignity and enterprise."[2]

Taylor's overarching goal for the new museum—to educate visitors about the history, culture, and accomplishments of the United States—profoundly influenced the ultimate architectural design of the building. Taylor's intellectual plan called for two large clusters of exhibits that would convey broad thematic stories spread across a vast period of time. "The Growth of America" series would outline the chronological development of U.S. society. The "Science and Technology in Industry" series would complement the historical chronology by presenting objects that recorded the nation's scientific achievements and technological accomplishments. Taylor wanted both of these large exhibitions to be centrally located, to serve as a broad overview of American history and as a general orientation to the museum.[3]

Taylor imagined that these two primary exhibits would occupy about a quarter of the new museum's total exhibition space. The remainder would be reserved to display the collections for which the Smithsonian had become famous. These included the national numismatic and philatelic collections, military and naval collections, the First Ladies' gowns, antique automobiles, and personal relics. Temporary, movable wall systems would allow the shape and size of the galleries to be modified as necessary to provide the most "successful, continuous, and flexible use of the building for many years into the future." In all, Taylor's plan included 460,000 square feet for public exhibitions with an additional 148,000 square feet reserved for collections storage.[4]

But Taylor's ambitious exhibition goals could only be realized if the overall physical design of the building provided visitors with a comfortable environment in which they could learn about America's past. No detail escaped Taylor's attention as he considered the needs of the five million people expected to come to the Museum each year. Smoking lounges, a cafeteria, air-conditioning, and windows to allow natural light into the building were amenities

considered key to a positive learning experience. Taylor envisioned wide and broad public corridors allowing visitors generous space to circulate freely throughout the building and providing easy access to exhibit galleries, with numerous escalators and elevators to move them between floors. Large, specially selected objects or key architectural features would provide landmarks for visitors to use as orientation devices as they moved throughout the building.[5]

Frank Taylor, the founding director of the Museum of History and Technology, inspects the construction site. His intellectual vision directly influenced the design of the building, including the central placement of the Star-Spangled Banner.

A LANDMARK INSTALLATION

The dramatic display of the Star-Spangled Banner was the linchpin of Taylor's grand vision. For the first time since its arrival at the Smithsonian, the entire flag would be displayed. It would hang on the second floor opposite the entrance from the National Mall, more than fifty feet in the air, as the centerpiece of the new building and as a proclamation of America's freedom. The Star-Spangled Banner would represent the Museum's commitment to history, while also providing visitors with a central landmark for physical orientation. Taylor wanted all of the Museum's visitors to begin their experience with the Star-Spangled Banner before

The Museum of History and Technology under construction on the National Mall, 1961.

moving on to the "Growth of America" exhibits located adjacent to it. For those who came in the Constitution Avenue entrance on the first floor, he wanted escalators positioned to carry them up to see the flag and begin their tour.

Responsibility for executing Taylor's plan for the new Museum of History and Technology was entrusted to Walker Cain, as lead architect for the firm of McKim, Mead and White. The architects adhered to Taylor's wishes faithfully, and his requirements for exhibition spaces and visitor amenities directly influenced the overall design of the building. To accommodate the large exhibition galleries, Cain selected a rectangular design with wide public corridors to allow easy movement between the wings of the building. Banks of escalators at each end carried visitors up and down between floors, and additional escalators in the center of the

The Museum of History and Technology, circa 1964.

first floor brought visitors directly up to see the Star-Spangled Banner as Taylor had envisioned. Cain created a truly monumental place of honor to present and display the flag. His central Flag Hall was three stories high, and the full flag was exhibited within its own recess of glazed blue tiles surrounded by a proscenium. Complementing the flag, a Foucault pendulum hung from the ceiling through an open oculus to the first floor, representing the technological achievements that were the other focus of the Museum's agenda.[6]

In September 1961, Smithsonian staff removed the flag from its display case in the Arts and Industries Building to prepare it for its move to the Museum of History and Technology. To prepare the flag for its new vertical mounting, workers laid the flag out on tables in the third-floor service court of the Arts and Industries Building. Specially woven two-inch-wide linen tapes were sewn at ten-inch intervals across the top of the linen backing, and the flag was returned to its case. Then in December 1963 the Star-Spangled Banner was folded carefully, loaded onto a truck, and driven across the Mall to its new home. Once inside Flag Hall, the flag was mounted on a forty-foot-high framework of three-inch aluminum tubing. The linen tapes on the flag's backing were affixed to a pipe at the top of the frame, and additional linen strips were sewn to the sides of the flag and safety-pinned to the diamond-patterned metal grid that covered the outer surface of the framework. The Star-Spangled Banner was protected from dust by a curtain of filtered air, which was blown in front of its entire surface from air diffusers that ran down the walls on either side of the recess. A false fly end with red and white stripes dyed to match the corresponding stripes on the flag was attached to the

Working from catwalks and
scaffolding, staff members
carefully hoist the flag into
position within the proscenium
arch, 1963.

grid below the flag's ragged fly end, and a false star was added in place of the missing one,
together leaving the visual impression of an intact flag.[7]

The new $36 million Museum of History and Technology opened its doors to rave reviews
in January 1964. *The Washington Post* proclaimed that the new museum was a "shrine" to the
rise of the United States as a nation, and *The Evening Star* described it as a "Palace of Progress." Visitors who entered from the Mall saw the Star-Spangled Banner towering in front of
them as they came through the doors, and school groups that arrived through the first-floor
bus entrance saw the flag slowly revealed to them as they ascended an escalator. Either way
one entered, the effect was dramatic. Observers noted that the Star-Spangled Banner occupied the "place of honor as the centerpiece" of the new museum and that the presentation
of the "frail" flag must elicit "some of the heart-stirring emotion that inspired Key to write

A school group in Flag Hall, 1995. From 1964 to 1998, the Star-Spangled Banner hung as a dramatic backdrop to public ceremonies, programs, and other special events.

the words of the National Anthem."[8] For the next thirty-four years the Star-Spangled Banner greeted visitors in Flag Hall and served as a backdrop for grand events marking the life of the nation. The Armistead family keepsake had become the Smithsonian's most recognizable icon as well as an acknowledged national treasure.

Moon landing. Photograph of Buzz Aldrin taken by Neil Armstrong, July 20, 1969.

ECOLOGY NOW!

Ecology poster. Inspired by antiwar activists who replaced the field of stars with a peace sign, environmentalists also altered the flag to make a political statement and promote their movement for a "greener" America.

MEANINGS AND MEMORIES THE FLAG

In July 1969 images of Apollo 11 astronauts planting the American flag on the moon signaled a proud and profound achievement for the nation and the world. Back on Earth, however, the Star-Spangled Banner was struggling to stay aloft in a strained and highly charged political atmosphere. During this decade of intense social divisions, the flag became a contested symbol of pride and protest in struggles over civil rights, foreign policy, and cultural values. Civil rights activists carried the American flag to pressure the nation to live up to its ideals of freedom and equality, while white segregationists flew Confederate flags to oppose the intervention of the federal government in their communities and to defend "the Southern way of life." In the

Jeans with flag patch. Many young Americans embraced the flag as a symbol of personal freedom. When a New Jersey teenager discovered in 1970 that she could not wear her favorite jeans to school because of a dress code that banned girls from wearing pants, she wrote to the American Civil Liberties Union for help defending her "right to free expression."

Stars-and-stripes lunch kit. Manufactured in 1970 by Aladdin Industries, Inc., of Nashville, Tennessee, this steel lunch kit appealed both to counterculture teens and patriotic construction workers.

IN THE SIXTIES

home-front battle over Vietnam, both sides used the flag to express their views about the morality and necessity of the war, sometimes with violent results.

Perhaps no issue epitomized the controversial nature of the American flag during the 1960s more than flag burning. When some burned the flag to protest government policies, others rushed to defend the flag from attack. State laws against flag desecration originally passed in the late 1800s were revived and enforced. In 1968, Congress passed the Federal Flag Desecration Law, making it a federal crime to "knowingly cast contempt upon any flag of the United States by publicly mutilating, defacing, defiling, burning, or trampling upon it."

After peaking in the late 1960s, however, the issue of flag desecration receded from the public spotlight. It would be revived twenty years later by the 1989 U.S. Supreme Court ruling in the case of *Texas v. Johnson*, which struck down all state and federal flag protection laws as violating the First Amendment right to free speech. Since then, politicians have made repeated efforts to amend the Constitution to prohibit flag burning, a move opposed by those who believe it would curtail essential civil liberties. As the debates over flag protection continue, memories of the turbulent 1960s continue to challenge and inspire Americans to contemplate the meaning of patriotism and the value of protest.

OPPOSITE
Demonstration against the Vietnam War. Washington, D.C., November 15, 1969.

BELOW
"Hard Hat" demonstration in support of the Vietnam War. New York City, 1970.

ABOVE
Selma Voting Rights March. Photograph by Matt Herron, 1965.

BELOW
Abbie Hoffman, Washington, D.C., 1968. Arrested for flag desecration after wearing an American flag shirt to protest the House Committee on Un-American Activities, the activist later proclaimed, "I regret that I have but one shirt to give for my country."[1]

SAVING THE
STAR-SPANGLED BANNER

Our role is to preserve [the Star-Spangled Banner] for the future, as it comes to us with all its history.
—Suzanne Thomassen-Krauss, Chief Conservator, Star-Spangled Banner Preservation Project, 2003

Museums struggle with inherent tensions between the need on the one hand to carefully protect and preserve objects for study and enjoyment by future generations, and the conflicting commitment on the other hand to share their collections with the public through display and exhibitions. The Smithsonian is no different. The American people place their trust in the Smithsonian to serve as a steward of the national collections, including the Star-Spangled Banner, but at the same time they expect to see the country's most beloved treasures on exhibit when they visit the Institution. Curators, conservators, collection managers, and exhibit designers strive to maintain the delicate balance between making the national collections available and accessible to the public and guarding them from the potentially harmful effects of long-term display.

Although the Smithsonian had taken many precautions over the decades to protect the Star-Spangled Banner, anxiety about the flag's fragile condition remained a constant. Soon after the opening of the Museum of History and Technology, responding to growing scientific knowledge about textile conservation, staff members discovered flaws in the new Flag Hall's display system. Without a protective enclosure, the flag's surrounding environment provided

Conservators cleaning the face of the flag at the National Museum of American History, 1982.

To protect the Star-Spangled Banner from exposure to light and debris, the Museum installed a movable screen in front of the flag in 1982. It was lowered hourly to reveal the flag.

neither stable humidity nor temperature, and the flag was constantly exposed to airborne pollution. In addition, the dramatic but difficult-to-maintain lighting system exposed the Star-Spangled Banner to inappropriately high light levels.

In January 1981 the Museum initiated a two-year conservation project in which the Star-Spangled Banner was carefully examined, and conservators working from scaffolding and cat-walks vacuumed the flag and its linen support. The area behind the flag was modified to reduce dust accumulation, the light levels were reduced, and changes to the air-handling system were made. From the visitor's point of view, however, the most important change was the installation of an opaque screen in front of the flag that was lowered once every hour to the accompaniment of a short program of two nineteenth-century arrangements of "The Star-Spangled Banner" played on historical band instruments and a brief narrative history of the flag. At these hourly intervals visitors had a brief but dramatic five-minute view of the flag. More important, the screen protected the flag from excessive exposure to light, dirt, and dust.[1]

But in 1994 one of the mechanisms that operated the protective screen failed, causing the screen to fall and drape in front of the flag, dangling by a single cable. Fortunately, the flag did not appear to suffer any damage as a result of the accident. Rather than reinstall the screen, the Museum took the opportunity to undertake a complete assessment of the flag's condition to better ensure its preservation far into the future. Thus began one of the most ambitious and complex textile conservation projects ever undertaken. The Museum faced the challenge of determining and executing the safest and most appropriate method to preserve a large textile that was originally made to last only a few short years. Now nearly two hundred years old and a national symbol and iconic treasure of the Smithsonian Institution, the Star-Spangled Banner merited whatever extraordinary measures were required to ensure its survival.

THE CALL TO ACTION

The National Museum of American History's effort to conserve and preserve the Star-Spangled Banner was unprecedented. To launch the initiative, the Museum convened in 1996 a group of fifty conservators, flag historians and curators, administrators, and scientists to consider options and develop a strategic plan of action. The two-day conference identified and discussed significant issues regarding the flag's preservation and future exhibition. Its findings and recommendations helped the Museum set the tone and direction for the entire preservation project.[2]

The conference acknowledged that this flag was no longer a "simple piece of military history." Given its role in the War of 1812 and its status as the inspiration for and the subject of the national anthem, the flag is a significant part of the country's national heritage. The Star-Spangled Banner is a powerful symbol to millions, representing the country's dreams, struggles, and achievements.[3] As the conference's recommendations reminded the Museum, the public is keenly interested in the fate of this flag and would want to know and understand

what would be done to care for and preserve it.[4] Most important, the conference cautioned the Museum to consider the goals and risks of any preservation activity carefully. What level of benefit could the Museum provide to the flag through its actions? Could the amount of time the Star-Spangled Banner remained on exhibition be extended through intervention and conservation? If so, could one quantify how much? Would the level of benefit be worth the potential risks to the flag and potential damage incurred by moving the flag and treating it? What posed the greater risk—moving and treating the flag or not doing anything at all? Ultimately, the conference issued a set of recommendations to the Museum, urging it to move forward with thorough analysis, caution, and respect.

Mindful of the conference's recommendations and based on the initial analysis of the flag's condition, the Museum made the decision to take the flag down from exhibition to examine and evaluate its condition. Based on those studies, the staff could then make further treatment decisions, including whether or not to remove the linen backing that flag preservationist Amelia Fowler had affixed to the flag in 1914, how to treat the flag to best preserve what strength remained, and how to display the flag for the Museum's millions of visitors in the future.[5]

To keep the public informed about the efforts to preserve the flag, the Museum developed a strategy to conduct the conservation treatment in full view of the public. The Museum had been designed and built around the Star-Spangled Banner, and the Museum wanted to share its activities with the public and provide them with assurance that the "flag was still there."[6] This proved to be among the most important decisions made throughout the course of the conservation project, for it provided an unprecedented opportunity to educate the public about the work conservators do to preserve the national collections. It also allowed the Smithsonian to uphold its pledge to Eben Appleton to keep the flag on view and not to remove it from the Institution.

To advise on future action, the Museum established an international technical advisory committee on the preservation of the flag. The Museum also formed an internal team of senior administrators, conservators, curators, educators, exhibit designers, historians, and public affairs specialists to manage, direct, and execute the research, preservation, and education outreach plans. Collectively, the group and its enterprises became known as the Star-Spangled Banner Preservation Project. The team was designed to be collaborative and meld the skills and talents of the diverse team members.

The Star-Spangled Banner Preservation Project was charged with four goals: to conduct the necessary research to understand the condition of the flag; to execute a conservation treatment program based on the knowledge gained from the research; to interpret the flag and educate the American public about its significance and symbolism; and to prepare the Star-Spangled Banner for its return to permanent display in the Museum, including the design of a new exhibition space that would provide the flag with the proper environment required to ensure its long-term health.[7]

By the summer of 1998 the National Museum of American History's plans to preserve the flag had gained national attention and earned important financial support. First Lady Hillary Rodham Clinton's White House Millennium Council and its Save America's Treasures program provided the critical leadership, bringing together core gifts from the U.S. Congress, the Pew Charitable Trusts, and Polo Ralph Lauren. On July 13, 1998, President William J. Clinton and First Lady Hillary Rodham Clinton joined Ralph Lauren at the Museum to announce his commitment of $10 million from Polo Ralph Lauren to the flag's conservation through the Save America's Treasures program. Additional support was received from the John S. and James L. Knight Foundation as well as through the donations of hundreds of individuals.[8] To help promote the story of the Star-Spangled Banner, the History Channel produced a television documentary and provided educational packets to teachers. The effort to save the Star-Spangled Banner had quickly become a true public-private partnership.

President William J. Clinton, Ralph Lauren, and First Lady Hillary Rodham Clinton at the launch of the Save America's Treasures program, July 13, 1998.

139

The flag was covered to protect it as it was removed and lowered from exhibition in December 1998.

The conservation team inspected and vacuumed the Star-Spangled Banner before moving it to the conservation laboratory in 1999.

THE FIRST STEPS

In December 1998 the flag was taken down and lowered into Flag Hall, where a temporary laboratory was constructed around it. The lowering of the flag was an enormous accomplishment in itself. After hanging for thirty-five years, the flag might not have the overall strength to withstand transport to the ground. Prior to taking it down, research was conducted to determine whether the flag's fibers were strong enough to endure the movement from the display position in Flag Hall. The analyses indicated that the Star-Spangled Banner was capable of withstanding such pressures, and a multifaceted team of engineers, conservators, and specialists in moving precious artifacts combined their skills and expertise to craft a plan to lower the flag safely on its display frame.

Once lowered, the flag was protected by a temporary laboratory constructed in Flag Hall, with windows in the walls that allowed the public to watch the work. Here, conservators examined the flag and the linen backing and drafted the first of many reports describing the flag's condition. Carefully examining and vacuuming the flag from a gantry (a movable bridge) that spanned the surface, conservators confirmed that the dyes in the network of stitches that Amelia Fowler's needlewomen had sewn over the flag had faded badly and that the linen backing had weakened with age. When the initial surveys and studies were completed, the flag was rolled onto a thirty-two-foot-long cylinder so it could be transported to a new two-thousand-square-foot conservation treatment facility. Rolling the Star-Spangled

Banner presented one of the most challenging activities undertaken by the project team and potentially one of the most hazardous to the flag. Rolling a textile may stress the object as it is wound around the rolling tube, but it would have been more problematic to move the flag in any other way. Given the flag's large size, care was taken to ensure that it was rolled evenly, with equal tension, to avoid distortions, tearing, and stress. Once rolled, the Star-Spangled Banner was crated for its short journey to its new home.

THE CONSERVATION LABORATORY

In February 1999 the Museum staff carefully moved the Star-Spangled Banner into a custom-designed conservation laboratory on the second floor. The new laboratory was specifically equipped to provide the best conditions possible for the Star-Spangled Banner during the preservation effort. The room was outfitted with its own dedicated heating, ventilation, and air-conditioning (HVAC) system to provide the flag with a stable environment and constant temperature and relative humidity. A series of filters removed pollutants and contaminants from the air, and a reverse-osmosis water-filtration system removed unwanted particles and chemicals from the water used to humidify the air. As light and water posed the greatest threats to the flag, special care was taken to limit their damaging effects. The filtered fluorescent lights were spaced around the edges of the room, and a suspended ceiling limited the amount of light reaching the flag. Instead of traditional water sprinklers, the chamber featured a gaseous fire-suppression system to protect the flag in the event of a fire emergency. In addition, the Museum installed several layers of security devices to protect the flag, including closed-circuit television cameras, motion detectors, and vibration sensors. All staff and visitors to the laboratory were required to change into "clean suits" and lab coats to limit the amount of contaminants brought into the room from the outside.

A series of connected portable stage platforms of the type normally used in theaters formed a large rectangular "table" on which the Star-Spangled Banner would rest throughout the conservation treatment. Across the breadth of the flag table was a gantry—a bridge with a thirty-two-foot-long span, seven feet in width, and weighing just over five thousand pounds. The gantry traveled on steel rails, like a railroad car, to carry the conservators and their equipment to any point along the flag for inspection and treatment. The gantry held task lighting, power outlets, vacuums, and chemical vapor extraction hoses to assist the conservators in whatever tasks were to be performed.

The conservation laboratory opened to the public on Memorial Day weekend in 1999. Its most striking feature was a fifty-foot-wide and twelve-foot-high plate glass wall that spanned one entire side of the laboratory. The glass wall allowed the Museum's visitors to be eyewitnesses to this unique and complex conservation project and introduced them to the science and art of conservation work. Visitors could see and appreciate the painstaking work of the conservators, who were often lying prone on their stomachs as they inspected and treated the flag. The viewing wall enabled the Smithsonian to uphold its pledge to Eben

The Conservation Research
and Treatment Laboratory

In 1999 the Star-Spangled Banner was moved into a special laboratory on the second floor of the National Museum of American History to undergo extensive conservation treatment. Custom-designed to provide a safe, clean environment for the thirty- by thirty-four-foot flag, the lab was constructed with a glass wall so visitors could watch the conservators working on the flag. This allowed the Museum to keep the Star-Spangled Banner on exhibition while educating the public about the important work conservators do to protect and preserve the national collections.

Support tables for flag. To protect the Star-Spangled Banner from the stress of its own weight, the flag was kept flat. The tables supporting the flag were actually modified stages topped with a special chemical-resistant surface. The total size of the support platform was thirty by thirty-six feet.

Rolling tube. This large tube allowed the flag to be moved or turned over safely. To move the banner out of Flag Hall, it was rolled onto the tube, encased in a break-apart crate, and taken into the new laboratory. Conservators also used the rolling tube to turn the flag over so the linen backing could be removed.

Fire-suppression system. Because water could damage the flag, the lab was protected by a gas fire-extinguishing system instead of a conventional sprinkler system.

Work gantry. A movable bridge, or gantry, suspended above the flag permitted easy access for examination and treatment. It could hold up to seven people at one time.

Track for gantry. Conservators pushed the gantry along the track to examine or work on different parts of the flag.

Exhaust hoses. The lab was equipped with its own heating, ventilation, and air-conditioning system (HVAC) that kept the air free of contaminants and maintained a steady temperature and relative humidity.

Support lab. Working on the Star-Spangled Banner itself was just one part of the extensive conservation effort. The support lab provided space and equipment for the conservation team to conduct tests, analyze findings, and document the work done on the flag.

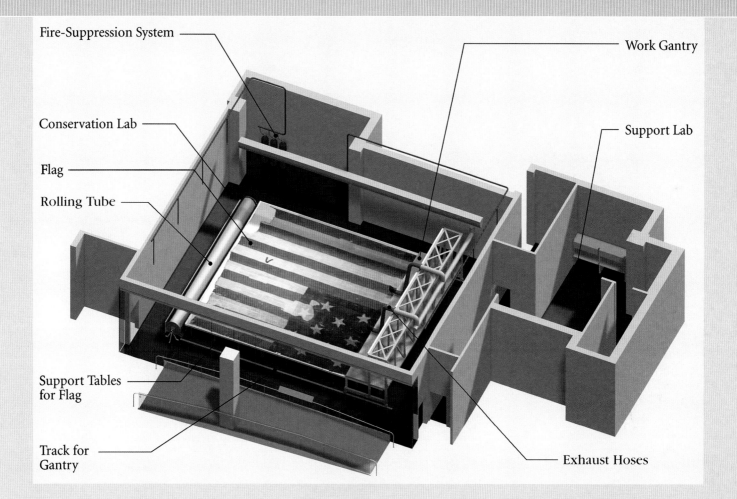

Fire-Suppression System

Conservation Lab

Flag

Rolling Tube

Support Tables
for Flag

Track for
Gantry

Work Gantry

Support Lab

Exhaust Hoses

Teams of conservators worked from the gantry, often lying prone on their stomachs, to inspect and treat the Star-Spangled Banner.

Appleton to keep the Star-Spangled Banner on view for the public to see and enjoy. Indeed, it was through the glass wall that visitors came to understand that the Star-Spangled Banner was not a mythical creation of Francis Scott Key's mind nor was it something of the past that had faded from memory. Instead, visitors could see firsthand that the flag described in the national anthem was a real artifact that could still be seen, studied, pondered, and appreciated.

Outside of the chamber the preservation team developed and installed a new exhibition, entitled "Preserving the Star-Spangled Banner," which placed the flag in the context of the War of 1812 and Key's moment of inspiration. For many visitors it was the first time they realized that the Star-Spangled Banner was not the flag supposedly made by Betsy Ross. Instead, the exhibition introduced the public to Mary Pickersgill and traced the stewardship of the flag from Lieutenant Colonel George Armistead and his descendants to the Smithsonian. In addition, the Star-Spangled Banner Preservation Project staff developed public programs and festivals to celebrate the flag and its history and engaged the public with weekly lectures and gallery talks describing the conservation process. For those who could not visit the Museum in person, the project's Web site provided regular updates on the conservation treatment.

THE TREATMENT PHASE

Textile conservation is a science carried out by highly skilled and highly trained practitioners called conservators. The goal of any conservation treatment is not to restore an object to its original condition but rather to stabilize the object and to halt or reduce further damage to the artifact. In making decisions regarding the treatment of an object, conservators must consider the physical and chemical makeup of the artifact, its purpose, how it was made and used, its current physical condition, the full history of the artifact, and all that it has endured. Though conservators take action to care for an object, they also must use care to ensure that nothing they do will adversely affect the object or prevent it from benefiting from newer conservation treatments and technologies that might arise in the future. As the Museum's visitors watched through the glass wall, the Star-Spangled Banner Preservation Project conservators executed the treatment plan inside the conservation laboratory. Using the information and results from the initial research and examination studies, the project's chief conservator and curators had mapped out a treatment plan for the flag that included removing the linen backing from 1914, removing harmful soils from the flag's surface, attaching the flag to new support materials, and identifying the optimum display environment for the flag when it would be returned to permanent exhibition. Visitors now saw this plan put into effect.

The conservation laboratory's fifty-foot-wide glass wall provided visitors with an unobstructed view of the treatment process.

145

The conservation team removing the 1.7 million stitches that held the linen support to the flag, 1999.

REMOVING THE LINEN SUPPORT

The first step in the process was the long and tedious task of removing the linen backing that Amelia Fowler and her staff had attached to the Star-Spangled Banner in 1914. Fowler's decision to attach the linen to the flag provided stability and support for the already frail and weak flag, and her work made it possible for the Star-Spangled Banner to remain on view for more than eighty years. But over time the backing had become weakened as well, and there was evidence that certain aspects of Fowler's treatment posed dangers to the flag. Fowler had imposed a uniform rectangular shape onto the Star-Spangled Banner as she attached it to the linen backing. Due to imperfections when it was originally made and because of its use as a garrison flag, the flag's edges are far from uniform, and its corners do not form perfect right angles. Fowler's forcing the flag into an unnatural shape placed undue stresses on the flag's fibers and yarns.

In addition, in order to display and support the flag in a vertical position, Fowler needed to apply 1.7 million stitches through the flag and the linen backing. This vast web of stitches put a great deal of stress on the flag as it hung on exhibition. While on view in Flag Hall, the flag was in constant but imperceptible motion. This movement caused continual rubbing, friction, and tension between the stitches and the Star-Spangled Banner's fibers, resulting in their weakening and breaking. Removing the linen backing would not only lessen the stress on the flag but also allow the conservators to perform further treatment procedures and better care for the Star-Spangled Banner. Dirt and oils could not be removed effectively with the linen still in place, but taking no action would result in further deterioration of the flag's fibers due to their chemical and physical interaction with the debris. Moreover, the linen stitches, individually dyed to mimic the flag's colors, obscured the true appearance of the flag. Removing the stitches and backing would allow the conservators to study both sides of the flag.[9] Some consultants cautioned the Museum that other flags had suffered damage when the stitches and support backings from similar conservation treatments were removed.[10] After weighing the expected benefit to the flag against the perceived risks, the Star-Spangled Banner Preservation Project team, in consultation with its international group of advisers and experts, elected to remove the linen backing from the flag.

The painstaking process of separating the Star-Spangled Banner from the linen took more than eighteen months. Beginning in May 1999, a team of conservators, working with clippers and tweezers, commenced on a long journey to undo the work Amelia Fowler and her team had completed more than eighty years before. Fowler had devised a stitching pattern that produced an intricate array of overlapping "cells." To remove the stitches, each "cell" had to be snipped in two places. The conservation team performed this work first seated in front of the flag on its rolling tube and later lying in a prone position on the gantry for up to six hours a day. The process was documented with photography and video recordings. Other research activities and routine tasks required to operate the laboratory filled the remainder of the conservators' time. While the Museum was open, the conservators performed their work under the enthralled gaze of millions of visitors. The clipping process was completed in March 2000—ten months after it began.

Conservators used clippers, scissors, and tweezers to carefully remove the stitches one by one.   147

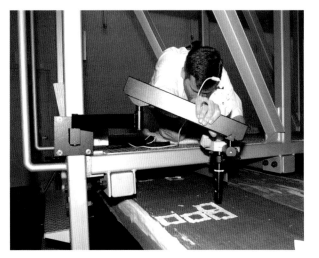

Detail spectrographic readings of the flag were taken to determine changes in color during treatment and to help select the most appropriate lighting for future exhibition.

Small test areas of the flag were studied and photographed to determine and measure changes in the flag as the result of treatment.

High-magnification SEM images captured the variety of airborne soils deposited on the flag.

BELOW
After removing the stitches and turning the flag over, the linen support is carefully lifted and cut away, 2000.

Between March and July 2000 the conservation team prepared to remove the linen backing. After another survey of the flag's surface, they rolled the Star-Spangled Banner onto its tube and then unrolled it with the linen support face up. Lying on the gantry and armed with scissors and tweezers, the conservators carefully pulled the clipped stitches and linen away from the flag. After six more months of meticulous work, the linen backing and the stitches had been completely removed. In February 2001 the Museum's visitors were able to see a side of the Star-Spangled Banner that had not been seen by the public since 1873. Visitors saw that the colors of the flag were much more vivid and vibrant than they had previously appeared. The faded stitches and gray soiling had obscured the flag's colors, causing a dingy and lackluster appearance. But the true colors of the Star-Spangled Banner had in fact retained much of their original intensity.

FROM SEWING TO SCIENCE

The Star-Spangled Banner was embedded with dust and debris from its years as an Armistead family keepsake and nearly a century of open, public exhibition. Modest attempts to clean the flag while it hung on view in the National Museum of American History's Flag Hall were necessarily cursory and did not include any dedicated and sophisticated studies of the contaminants on the Star-Spangled Banner. With the stitches and linen backing removed and the flag in a proper laboratory, the conservation team was able to use the latest advances in science and technology to help them understand the condition of the flag and identify the best means and methods of removing harmful contaminants.

To begin, the scientists and conservators used advanced scientific equipment and processes to assess the relative strength of the flag's fibers and to determine the level of risk posed by the presence of contaminants in the flag. The high degree of deterioration in the fibers (the white, or undyed, fibers showed more deterioration than the red or the blue) was attributed to its use at Fort McHenry and its exposure to light over the years. Additional scientific investigations revealed a number of foreign materials and stains on the flag, caused by dye transfers and contact with water, oil, and greasy liquids. There were other stains caused by resinous materials like tar, possibly paint, and waxlike compounds. Further, and perhaps more problematic, were the lipids and oily and fatty films found in the flag. Over time these substances could create chemical reactions that could potentially harm the flag. Removal

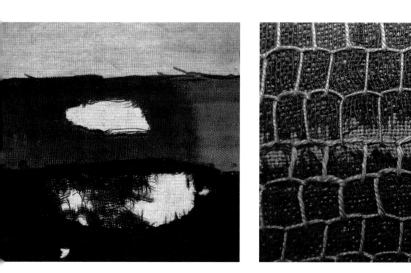

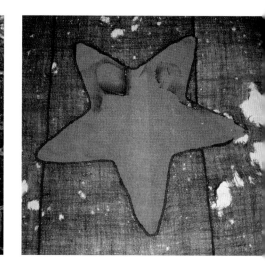

of these deposits would prevent the further deterioration of the flag's fragile fibers. High-magnification images produced by a scanning electron microscope (SEM) and research techniques such as confocal microscopy enabled the conservators and other scientists to determine that the fibers of the flag, although stable, were particularly fragile due to chemical deterioration, abrasions, and stresses.

Before proceeding with any cleaning process, the conservation team evaluated whether the process of removing the contaminants from the flag would also remove historical evidence embedded in it. Once again, SEM images, combined with energy-dispersive spectroscopy (EDS), allowed researchers to identify the specific elements on the flag. Other scientific investigations revealed a number of foreign materials embedded in the flag, including organic compounds combined with sodium, magnesium, calcium, and iron. Significant levels of chlorine and sulfur, with traces of phosphate, aluminum, and silicon, were also found. The conservation team determined that there were no identifiable soils with historical significance in or on the flag and particularly no evidence of the Battle of Baltimore that would be removed by the proposed cleaning technique. The remaining challenge to resolve was determining how to clean the flag without causing additional damage.

CLEANING THE FLAG

In August 2001 the conservation team began to remove the debris from the flag using common cosmetic sponges. This was a "dry" process to remove debris first without the use of water or organic solvents. Lying face-down on the gantry, the conservators passed over the flag inch by inch, gently blotting the surface of the flag to collect and remove debris. The material removed from the flag was tested to ensure that only modern contaminants were removed. The dry-sponge cleaning was completed in March 2002, with the conservators using more than ten thousand sponges to clean both sides of the flag. Photographs comparing the flag before and after this treatment clearly illustrate that the appearance of the flag was improved and the number of particles on the flag had been reduced.

Despite the success of the dry-sponge cleaning, however, a significant amount of debris, including oils and mold, remained on the flag, indicating that further treatment with some sort of solution would be required. Early research showed that the use of water to treat these wool fibers would remove soluble proteins and cause microfractures in the fibers of the flag.

Investigations and treatment revealed many foreign substances in the flag, such as this greasy, waxlike stain found on the hoist (rope) sleeve.

Insects caused numerous small holes in the flag.

The stain on this star resulted from contact with corroded iron, probably a metal buckle.

149

Conservators carefully blotted the surface of the flag to remove debris while protecting the fragile fibers and yarns of the Star-Spangled Banner. More than ten thousand ordinary cosmetic sponges were used to clean the flag.

But there was also concern that the use of organic solvents might desiccate and weaken the woolen fibers, and could pose a serious health risk to the conservators using them. Instead, the conservation team considered using a solvent comprised primarily of acetone mixed with a small amount of water. But would treatment using such a mixture cause more damage to the flag and outweigh the expected benefit?

Research tests were conducted in July and August 2002 to study the effects of cleaning using water, acetone, or a mixture of acetone and water on the fibers of the flag. The project team rejected other solvents from consideration as being too hazardous for use. Tests on small fibers taken directly from the Star-Spangled Banner indicated that the use of water alone would not be an acceptable treatment solution. The greasy and oily material on the flag was not the type of soiling cleanable by water and would require the addition of detergents to remove the deposits. If water alone was ineffective and the use of organic solvents posed hazards, would an acetone and water mixture be safe and effective?

The project's Technical Advisory Group (TAG) met in late August 2002 to discuss the potential risks and rewards of further treatment to the flag and to provide counsel regarding the proposed treatment of the flag with a solvent mixture. To arrive at a recommendation, the TAG addressed three fundamental questions. First, would solvent cleaning have a long-term beneficial impact on the stability of the flag? Second, would the acetone and water treatment itself be harmful to the flag by leaching the internal lipids, proteins, and oils from the fibers in the flag and thus contributing to future instability? Finally, they asked, was it absolutely critical to perform this treatment now, or would it be possible to treat the flag at a later time with the same level of effectiveness?

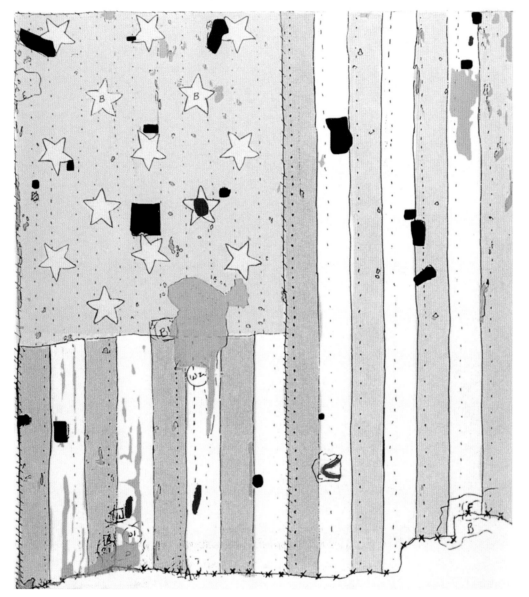

This color graphic was created to document the location of patches and major losses in the flag.

Research continued through February 2003 to answer these questions. A selection of yarns from the flag was divided into individual test groups. The first group of yarn samples was cleaned with the solvent mixture. A second group of yarns was divided again, artificially aged five, twenty-five, fifty, and seventy-five years, and then cleaned with the solvent mixture. Each of these groups of fibers was tested to measure the effect of both aging and cleaning on the strength and mechanical structure of the yarns. The results of these tests were measured against two separate control groups of yarns—one group that had been artificially

The Star-Spangled Banner's New Image

In June 2002, in celebration of Flag Day, the National Museum of American History released a new composite image of one of the Smithsonian's most revered objects—the Star-Spangled Banner. Among the many achievements of the Star-Spangled Banner Preservation Project in studying, researching, cleaning, and stabilizing the flag, the creation of this new photograph ranked as a milestone event.

This new image revealed the true condition of the Star-Spangled Banner. Earlier photographs, taken when the Star-Spangled Banner was hanging on a reproduction backing, obscured tears, earlier repairs, and the cutting of "souvenir" pieces that the flag had suffered before becoming part of the national collections. As part of the conservation treatment, conservators removed the linen backing applied by Amelia Fowler, which had distorted the true shape, condition, and appearance of the flag. Behind the linen was a side of the Star-Spangled Banner that had not been visible for nearly a hundred years and had never been photographed before. The fibers on this side of the flag were less soiled and had been partially protected from sunlight and fading, and the new photography captured the vibrancy of the flag's colors. But it also dramatically revealed how delicate and vulnerable the flag truly was. As such, this new image presented a vastly different view of the Star-Spangled Banner than the public had ever seen.

Photographing the flag in its conservation laboratory posed enormous challenges for the Smithsonian photographers. Working inside the laboratory, they could not position themselves far enough away to capture the thirty- by thirty-four-foot flag in a single frame. Instead, they took seventy-three individual, high-resolution photographs of specific portions of the flag using a Hasselblad camera mounted on the rolling gantry—a movable bridge normally used by the conservators to treat the flag. Each image covered forty-four square inches of the flag. Computer technology assembled and joined the individual images into a single, composite photograph.

The new composite image of the flag is a historical document in its own right. It speaks to the Star-Spangled Banner's unique history, its age, its inherent fragility, and the effort to preserve the flag that had inspired the national anthem.

OPPOSITE
Final composite image of the
Star-Spangled Banner.

TOP LEFT
One of seventy-three photographs
used to create the composite
image of the Star-Spangled
Banner, this shot corresponds to
the square located in Column 2,
Row F on the grid diagram at
lower right.

BOTTOM LEFT
Smithsonian photographers
worked from the gantry to take
images of the Star-Spangled
Banner.

BOTTOM RIGHT
The Star-Spangled Banner
was mapped and divided into
eight columns and nine rows
to provide a grid reference for
all photography and treatment
documentation.

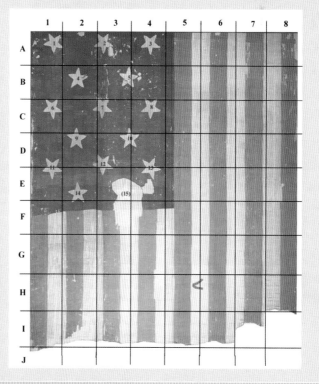

153

To support the Star-Spangled Banner and keep fragile areas in place, conservators sewed a lightweight polyester material, called Stabiltex, to the back of the flag. This photograph shows a white stripe secured to the Stabiltex backing and a red stripe in the process of being stabilized.

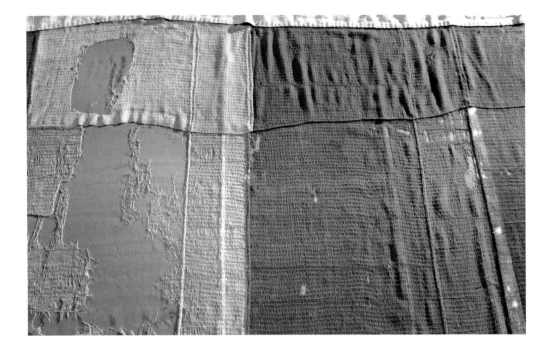

aged, but not cleaned, and a final group that had neither been aged nor cleaned with the solvent mixture. A second phase of research examined fibers from these same yarns to identify any adverse internal changes to the yarns as the result of the treatment.[11]

The research findings indicated that treatment with the solvent mixture would benefit the flag by slightly increasing the mechanical strength of the yarns as measured by the amount of force required to break an individual yarn after treatment. Further, the test data indicated that there would be no internal physical or chemical changes to the fibers (weakening or stiffening) as a result of the cleaning procedure. The solvent cleaning itself would not adversely impact the flag. Rather, by removing the oily particulates, some flexibility would be restored, making the fibers less susceptible to abrasions and breaking caused by brittle fibers rubbing against one another.

The aging studies revealed that there was an extremely narrow window of time in which to make a decision to treat the flag. The results suggested that the proposed treatment would benefit the flag only if undertaken within the next five years—it would not benefit the flag if deferred longer than that time. In April 2003 the Technical Advisory Group, despite understandable concern and reservation, affirmed the project's decision to move forward with the solvent mixture treatment. The treatment proposal for cleaning the Star-Spangled Banner with the solvent mixture was presented to senior National Museum of American History staff in September 2003 and approved by the Museum's director.

The treatment itself began in October 2003 and continued through March 2004. A single row of table surfaces was replaced with a row of aluminum frames stretched with polyester mesh. With the flag extended over the frames, the solvent mixture was brushed onto the surface. Acid-free blotter paper absorbed the solvent mixture and the contaminants as the liquid passed through the fibers of the Star-Spangled Banner. After the cleaning, color readings were made with a spectrophotometer verifying that the colors of the flag were not altered but that soils were removed.

FINAL STEPS

With the solvent mixture treatment completed, the conservation team then turned their attention to the stresses and tears in the flag created by the 165 repairs made previously to the Star-Spangled Banner. Thirty of the most damaging and most disfiguring mends were removed, and the areas were treated in order to realign them back to their original positions. These procedures reduced the stress on the flag and improved its physical appearance. The entire flag was photographed, including each stain and mend in the flag, details of the flag's construction, and other items of interest to curators and historians.

The final phase of work on the flag was the attachment of a new material that would support and protect the Star-Spangled Banner while on future exhibition. Although it was clear that the flag could never be hung vertically again (nor would the Smithsonian ever attempt to exhibit it in that way), it still needed to be physically stabilized for exhibition. Modern materials offered the conservation team improved options that had not been available to Amelia Fowler in 1914. The conservation team opted to use Stabiltex, a strong, stable, and almost sheer material that would provide the necessary support. To minimize the amount of stitching, the conservation team began attaching the flag to the Stabiltex along the existing seams of the flag. In other, weaker areas where there was more damage, conservators used a couching stitch to stabilize the flag. The conservators completed the attachment of the Star-Spangled Banner to the Stabiltex in September 2004.

The attachment of the Stabiltex to the flag marked a significant moment in the flag's history. The Smithsonian, with the assistance of an international team of conservators, engineers, scientists, and other consultants—and with financial support from hundreds of individuals, corporations, and organizations—had succeeded in its mission to stabilize the historic flag and retard its further deterioration. But the successful execution and completion of the conservation treatment represented only half of the overall preservation effort. The final challenge remained: to build a new home for the Star-Spangled Banner that would ensure its continued preservation while also making it accessible to the public. Even as the conservators and scientists concluded their work to save the flag from further deterioration in 2005, architects, exhibit designers, conservators, curators, and engineers were combining their efforts to design a new, permanent home for the flag that would preserve it for future generations to see.

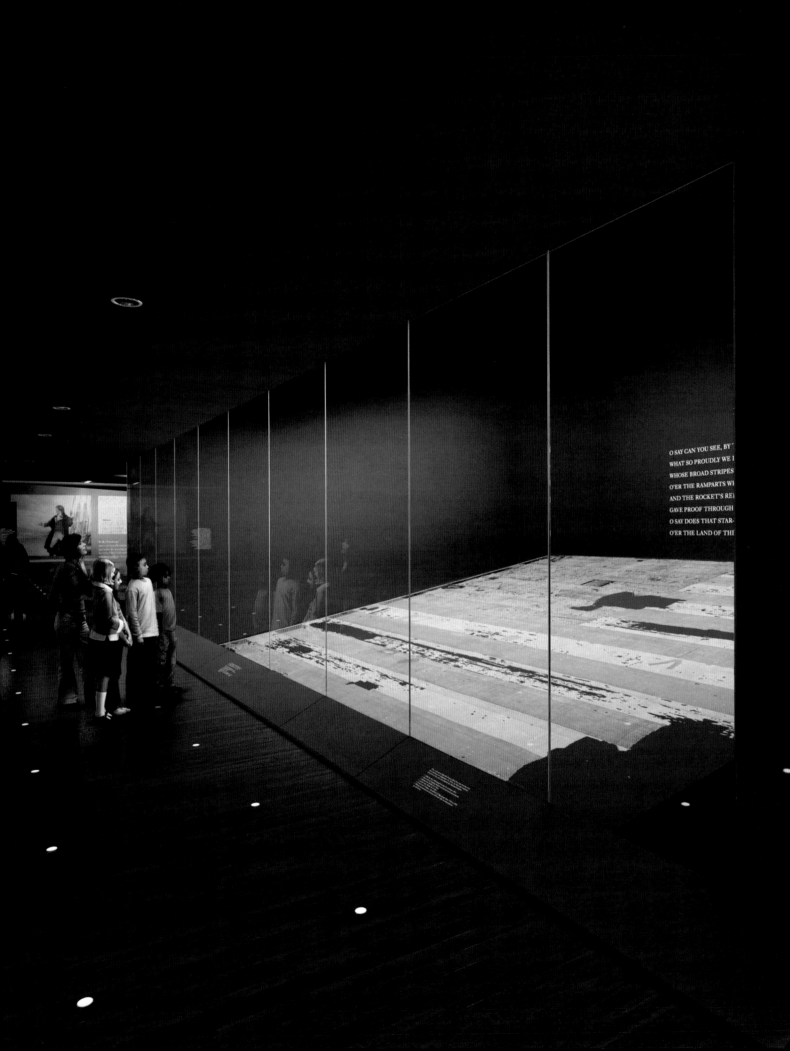

O SAY CAN YOU SEE, BY
WHAT SO PROUDLY WE
WHOSE BROAD STRIPES
O'ER THE RAMPARTS WH
AND THE ROCKET'S RE
GAVE PROOF THROUGH
O SAY DOES THAT STAR-
O'ER THE LAND OF THE

A NEW HOME FOR
AN ENDURING ICON

So, as you see this flag, and leave this place, promise yourself that when your great-grandchildren are here, they'll not only be able to see the Star-Spangled Banner—it will mean just as much to them then as it does to you today.

—President William J. Clinton, July 13, 1998

The National Museum of American History was constructed around the Star-Spangled Banner. When the Museum opened in 1964, the flag hung proudly in Flag Hall as the Museum's central icon and welcoming point for visitors. The return of the Star-Spangled Banner to the heart of the Museum in 2008 was a monumental engineering and design effort fusing the talents, knowledge, and skills of countless architects, conservators, curators, educators, engineers of all disciplines, designers, historians, and construction workers. Preserved and protected, the Star-Spangled Banner once again occupies its central place in the National Museum of American History.

TRANSFORMING AMERICA'S MUSEUM

At the same time that the Star-Spangled Banner team began to consider a new home for the flag, the National Museum of American History was embarking upon a monumental renovation and transformation. On June 29, 2001, the Smithsonian's Board of Regents took the first step, appointing a Blue Ribbon Commission to review all aspects of the Museum's operations, including the physical state of the building, and to provide a roadmap to guide the Museum's future renovation and transformation.[1]

The new Star-Spangled Banner chamber protects the flag with the optimum environmental conditions required for its long-term preservation while providing the Museum's visitors a dramatic encounter with the flag.

In many respects the Blue Ribbon Commission's report echoed the concerns expressed half a century earlier by Leonard Carmichael and Frank Taylor. Part of the impetus to create the Museum of History and Technology had stemmed from the desire to teach visitors about the American values of freedom, democracy, and industry in the face of the perceived communist threat. Likewise, in the wake of the September 11 terrorist attacks and with a renewed sense of patriotism, the Blue Ribbon Commission affirmed in its report the critical need to educate Americans and the people of the world about the ideals of freedom, democracy, and opportunity that are so commonly associated with what it has meant to be "American." But the Blue Ribbon Commission warned that it would be impossible to understand the evolution of these ideals and their various meanings, and thus to understand who Americans are as a people, without a proper understanding of U.S. history. The commission concluded that "a well-informed sense of American history is of obvious importance. And the National Museum of American History has a fundamental role to play in helping Americans develop that well-informed sense."[2]

The Blue Ribbon Commission found that many of the elements that were considered essential to the original plan of the building—both in its intellectual and in its physical organization—had become muddled as the Museum evolved during its first forty years. Much like the Arts and Industries Building in the 1950s, the National Museum of American History had become cluttered in its attempts to meet the ever-increasing demands for exhibition space. The commission's candid critique once again used the unfortunate metaphor of the "attic" to describe the jumbled conditions.[3] Taylor had seen the vast size of the new Museum of History and Technology as essential to telling a comprehensive story about American history, but now that enormous scale was viewed as an impediment to providing the visitor with a coherent experience.

Despite the daunting challenges, the commission strongly argued that the National Museum of American History could address the issues successfully and "retain its special place of trust within American culture, . . . sustain its unrivaled position as a repository for American historical collections, and . . . remain one of the most visited museums in the world."[4] The commission urged the Museum to remove exhibit cases that were cluttering the public corridors and provide visitors with better orientation through the opening up of the multistory central core—providing clear lines of sight throughout the Museum would allow visitors to find where they wanted to go. The commission urged the increased use of natural and artificial light, and the placement of large, landmark objects at the end of each public corridor was encouraged to help visitors orient themselves within the building.[5] And finally, the commission urged the Museum to return the Star-Spangled Banner "as a central icon . . . to the visible core of the museum." Although "special measures must (and will) be taken to assure the flag is preserved and protected," the commission specified that the Star-Spangled Banner must "be highly visible."[6]

The challenge of conceiving and executing a plan to renovate and reinvigorate the National Museum of American History was given to the architectural firm of Skidmore, Owings & Merrill and Turner Construction Company. Design firms C&G Partners and Chermayeff & Geismar Studio provided the conceptual development for the display of the Star-Spangled Banner and collaborated on the design of the new permanent gallery. After years of design and planning, the National Museum of American History closed its doors to the public on September 5, 2006, and began the process of physically transforming the building.[7]

Much of the renovation was dedicated to updating the building's decaying infrastructure and improving the visitor services essential to operating a national museum visited by millions each year, but its success has hinged on incorporating the recommendations of the Blue Ribbon Commission and creating new ways for the Museum to present the objects of the nation's past. Responding to the call to reduce clutter and to improve visitor orientation, several dramatic architectural changes were made to the building's central core. Most notably, a vast skylight bathes visitors in natural light as they congregate in the new central atrium, helping to create a brighter, warmer, more inviting atmosphere in the heart of the Museum. A monumental glass staircase reestablishes the primary connection between the Museum's main two floors. The large marble panels that surrounded the old Flag Hall on the third floor were removed, creating grand vistas across the Museum and allowing visitors on the third floor to look down into the Flag Hall for the first time. To showcase the collections, the Museum installed 275 linear feet of "artifact walls" in the public corridors.

THE NEW STAR-SPANGLED BANNER CHAMBER

The crowning achievement of the renovation is the reinstallation of the Star-Spangled Banner in a chamber in the ceremonial heart of the Museum. "The Star-Spangled Banner is one of our nation's most treasured objects, a symbol of what this country stands for," stated the Museum's director, Brent D. Glass. "Its new surroundings are part of a strategic plan to ensure the long-term preservation of the flag, revitalize the museum, . . . and help future generations experience what it means to be an American."[8] The creation of a new and permanent home for the Star-Spangled Banner posed three major engineering and intellectual challenges. First, the new display chamber must provide the environmental conditions required to preserve the flag. Second, the new exhibition gallery must present the context in which the flag earned its historical significance. And finally, though the flag itself would not be visible in Flag Hall, the design of the new chamber and exhibition gallery must continue to serve as the central focal point for visitors' museum experience. The new flag chamber and gallery elegantly and dramatically address these challenges, ensuring the long-term preservation of the flag while providing enhanced access for the public.

The most significant difference between the new Star-Spangled Banner exhibition and its original display in the Museum is that the flag no longer hangs vertically in Flag Hall.

This architectural rendering depicts the major components of the renovated National Museum of American History, including a skylight to allow natural light into the building, artifact walls to showcase the collections, a grand staircase to connect the first and second floors, the abstract flag as the focal point in Flag Hall, and the flag chamber and exhibition— the new home for the Star-Spangled Banner.

161

Once the linen backing was removed, it was evident that the Star-Spangled Banner had been exposed to significant stress, pollutants, and damage from light. The Museum recognized that, given the flag's frail condition, it could never be returned to its original position hanging beneath the proscenium arch in Flag Hall. For the long-term safety and preservation of the artifact, the Museum decided to display the flag within a secure and environmentally controlled chamber. The chamber is a near-two-story, isolated structure situated on the second floor in Flag Hall. A section of the third-floor slab was removed to make way for it. All of the existing mechanical systems, air ducts, and plumbing were removed during the renovation and redirected so as not to pass over the top of the flag chamber—this protects against leaks or possible damage due to maintenance work being performed over the flag chamber.

Controlling the environment within the chamber is of the utmost importance to the long-term preservation of the flag. The chamber has been designed and constructed to be air-, light-, and watertight. It is equipped with a dedicated heating, ventilation, and air-conditioning (HVAC) unit to provide the stringent control of humidity and temperature essential to the flag's preservation. Uncontrolled changes in temperature and humidity pose threats to most objects in the Museum's collections but are particularly dangerous to the Star-Spangled Banner. Rapid fluctuations in humidity could cause the individual fibers of the flag to swell (if too humid) or become brittle (if too dry) and break. The HVAC unit also maintains positive air pressure in the space to prevent contaminants from seeping into the room from the outside. All of the air that enters the chamber is heavily filtered to remove particles, chemicals, and biological agents. The HVAC system also includes alarms to alert Museum staff to spikes in the temperature or humidity within the chamber. As part of the design and engineering process, computer programs were used to model and predict the path of airflow in the space to prevent strong airflows from passing directly over or through the flag, which could cause damage over long periods of time.

As was the case in the previous conservation laboratory, the new flag chamber requires a coordinated display table and gantry system to facilitate conservators' access to the flag for future examinations and treatments. The aluminum display table is more than thirty feet wide and thirty-four feet long and weighs approximately seven thousand pounds. The surface of the table is comprised of perforated, four-foot-square aluminum panels. The architectural support fabric (to which the Stabiltex backing of the Star-Spangled Banner is attached) is held to the table with a series of clamps underneath the table's edge, out of view of the public. In addition, in areas of great loss in the flag, the architectural fabric is stitched to the table through the many perforations in its surface.

While on public display, the flag and the table will be raised at a ten-degree angle. In this position the top edge of the flag will rise approximately eight feet in the air, offering a dramatic view to the visitor. But for inspections and cleaning, conservators must be able to move the table and the flag to a horizontal position. The table is thus moved through a series of hand-operated gears and shifts in a gentle manner to prevent vibrations and movement of the flag. The accompanying gantry is strong and stable enough to support the work of up to three conservators without vibrations that would prevent the use of microscopes or other sensitive equipment. They can move the gantry by pushing it along tracks hidden underneath the table. When not in use, it is placed in a "garage" at the rear of the chamber, hidden by the flag in its display position.

To protect against the threat of fire, all sources of possible ignition—electrical power, outlets, or items requiring electricity, such as the lighting fixtures—are kept outside of the chamber. The operation of the table and gantry are completely mechanical and move without electrical power. Because water also presents a grave threat to the flag, the Star-Spangled Banner team selected an alternative to traditional sprinkler systems to protect the flag from fire. Rather than relying on water or gas to put out a fire, the fire-prevention system prohibits any sort of combustion in the chamber by reducing the concentration of oxygen. This solution also poses less risk to the flag than a fire-suppression system that would discharge large amounts of gas across the flag at very high velocities. In addition, the Museum has installed multiple layers of security systems, alarms, closed-circuit television cameras, and other devices to protect the Star-Spangled Banner, the flag chamber, and the adjoining exhibit spaces.

Over the long term the greatest threat to the flag is exposure to light. The flag's fibers absorb the energy from light, which causes harmful chemical reactions and deterioration. To reduce the amount of damage, the amount of light used to illuminate the flag is severely restricted. Thus selecting the best method of lighting the flag and the surrounding exhibition gallery posed a significant challenge. Different types of lighting present different risks and benefits to the flag that must be weighed and balanced. While the chamber currently uses digital projectors and filtered, metal halide bulbs, research continues into the development of a light-emitting diode (LED) lighting system through which specific wavelengths of light may be selected to illuminate the flag, thereby reducing the long-term damage to the Star-Spangled Banner.

Ultimately, although the functionality of a laboratory is still required in the new chamber, the look and feel must be very different. During the conservation phase of work, the flag was displayed on a flat surface in a laboratory. All of the room's specialized systems to control the temperature and humidity, the low lighting, the gaseous fire-suppression system, security devices, and the gantry were in clear view of visitors, drawing attention to the conservation process. In contrast, the new chamber has been designed to engage visitors in the story and significance of the flag. The multiple mechanical and technical systems have been integrated into the design of the chamber to provide long-term care for the flag but without the visible clutter, equipment, and other visual distractions of the laboratory. Instead, the Star-Spangled Banner is now presented in a simple, elegant, and uncluttered setting as befits a national treasure.

The abstract flag serves as the Museum's focal point and announces the entrance to the Star-Spangled Banner chamber and exhibition.

PLACING THE STAR-SPANGLED BANNER IN ITS HISTORICAL CONTEXT

But it is not enough to preserve the Star-Spangled Banner. It is more than a mere historical relic; it is a national symbol rooted in a critical moment in the nation's history. When it hung in Flag Hall, the Star-Spangled Banner was essentially a dramatic centerpiece, presented with little or no historical context. Today, however, that is no longer the case. The Star-Spangled Banner gallery presents the flag in the context of history, exploring its legacy as a national symbol.

The exhibition at the entrance to the chamber centers on the morning of September 14, 1814, when U.S. soldiers at Baltimore's Fort McHenry raised a huge American flag to celebrate a crucial victory over British forces during the War of 1812. The United States was at war with England, the greatest power in the world, and the young nation was struggling for its survival. Charred timber from the White House (burned by the British), a fragment of an exploded British bombshell, a Congreve rocket, and other artifacts document the nation's struggle and its perseverance. After American forces withstood the British attack at the Battle of Baltimore, the sight of those "broad stripes and bright stars" inspired Francis Scott Key to write the song that eventually became America's national anthem.

As visitors turn to enter the flag-viewing area, they have their first glimpse of the flag as Key did in the "dawn's early light." Designed to be contemplative and respectful, the viewing area provides an unobstructed view of the Star-Spangled Banner through a forty-eight-foot-wide wall of floor-to-ceiling glass. When the Star-Spangled Banner previously hung high in the air in Flag Hall, it was impossible for visitors to examine the flag closely. With the crowds of people congregating in front of it, the Star-Spangled Banner was perceived more often as a backdrop instead of a treasure of national significance. The new flag chamber allows visitors to see the Star-Spangled Banner up close and provides an opportunity to view the flag devoid of clutter, equipment, and other visual distractions.

On the back wall above the flag the first stanza of the national anthem appears dramatically in backlit letters. The flag that visitors now see on display has a strikingly different appearance from the Star-Spangled Banner visitors encountered in the Museum before the preservation effort. No effort has been made to restore the flag to its original condition, to camouflage the damage, or to make it look "like new." The ragged edges, patches, and holes are plainly visible. The flag is shown in its true condition, allowing visitors to see it as an artifact as well as an icon—as a treasured piece of American history. Although its stripes are tattered and its stars faded, the flag endures: it is, indeed, still here. Just as it inspired Francis Scott Key two centuries ago, the Star-Spangled Banner inspires Americans today to reflect on the ideals that unite us, the experiences we share, and the heritage we hold in trust for future generations. Upon leaving the viewing area, visitors pass through a gallery that explores the history and legacy of the Star-Spangled Banner as a flag, a song, and a symbol. Through period graphics, objects, audio, and video presentations, visitors learn about Mary Pickersgill and the making of the Star-Spangled Banner, the Armistead family's care for it in the

nineteenth century, and the Smithsonian Institution's stewardship of the banner since 1907. An audio presentation helps visitors learn how Francis Scott Key's song roused a nation's spirits during the War of 1812 and how Americans throughout the generations since have adapted the song to suit the times, expressing their cultural tastes as well as their patriotism. The concluding section of the gallery explores the American flag as arguably the country's most significant national symbol, invested with many meanings and memories. Ever since Key wrote his song in 1814, in times of celebration and crisis, pride and protest, the flag has continued to wave as a symbol of the nation, its people, and the ideals for which it stands.

THE ABSTRACT FLAG

To take the place of the Star-Spangled Banner in Flag Hall, the Museum has installed an abstract flag representing, but not replicating, the Star-Spangled Banner. This monumental exhibit element appears to wave majestically in the air, providing a new visual and architectural focal point for the Museum and heralding the entrance to the Star-Spangled Banner exhibition. At nearly forty feet long and comprised of fifteen individual stripes, it echoes the design of the Star-Spangled Banner and pays respect to the history it represents. Each stripe is comprised of individual pixels of mirrored polycarbonate that catch and reflect the movement of light and people in the Museum, creating a mosaic of colors and shapes. Just as the American flag evokes different meanings and values to every person, what each person sees in the abstract flag will also be unique.

LONG MAY IT WAVE

The installation of the Star-Spangled Banner in its new flag chamber marked the successful conclusion of the Smithsonian's monumental effort to preserve its treasured artifact. The garrison flag that became the Star-Spangled Banner was not intended to be used for more than a few years at most, and Mary Pickersgill would surely be surprised to see the flag she made so long ago preserved and displayed with such reverence today. This ordinary flag, assembled inside of a brewery, has been transformed from a personal family keepsake to an extraordinary and transcendent national treasure. Visitors who see the Star-Spangled Banner today share a moment of the past with Francis Scott Key, Lieutenant Colonel George Armistead, Georgiana Armistead Appleton, Eben Appleton, and all of the people in the succeeding generations who have treasured this great flag and helped to preserve it.

Beginning with the Star-Spangled Banner, the symbolism and meanings of the American flag have evolved as we have changed as a people. Generations of Americans have invested the flag with their own meanings and memories. Though most may agree that the flag represents the American values of freedom, liberty, and equality, what many think of as "America" is dynamic and does not conform to any single definition. The flag has been raised in celebration and in protest, its meaning discussed and debated but never irrelevant. The flag simultaneously embodies what we aspire to be as a people and a nation and the understanding that

those ideals will never be perfectly realized. It instructs us about our past while challenging us to create a "more perfect" America in the future. Through its preservation efforts, the National Museum of American History ensures that future generations will be able to see the Star-Spangled Banner and learn these critical lessons. This is why saving the Star-Spangled Banner is important.

The Star-Spangled Banner's broad stripes and bright stars, although somewhat faded, still remind us of that September morning in 1814 when Key wrote the words that are now so familiar to all Americans. When Key declared that "our flag was still there," he fused the physical symbol of the nation with universal feelings of patriotism, courage, and resilience. The flag was no longer just an emblem of the nation; it became a representation of the country's values and the ideals for which it stands. This is what gives the Star-Spangled Banner its unbounded resonance and value beyond measure. As President William J. Clinton so eloquently put it at the launch of the Save America's Treasures program in 1998, "this Star-Spangled Banner and all its successors have come to embody our country, what we think of as America."[9]

Preserved for future generations, the Star-Spangled Banner will continue to inspire visitors in its new home at the National Museum of American History.

NOTES

Introduction

Epigraph: President William J. Clinton, launching the Save America's Treasures campaign at the National Museum of American History (hereafter, NMAH), on July 13, 1998.

1. Edward S. Delaplaine, *Francis Scott Key: Life and Times* (New York: Biography Press, 1937), 99–100.

Chapter 1: The Battle of Baltimore

Epigraph: "A Republican paper of Boston" is quoted in *Niles' Weekly Register*, October 1, 1814.

1. For discussion of the British motivations for attacking Washington and Baltimore, see Donald R. Hickey, *The War of 1812: A Forgotten Conflict* (Urbana: University of Illinois Press, 1989), 194; Anthony S. Pitch, *The Burning of Washington: The British Invasion of 1814* (Annapolis, Md.: Naval Institute Press, 1998), 29; Joseph A. Whitehorne, *The Battle for Baltimore* (Baltimore, Md.: The Nautical and Aviation Publishing Company of America, 1997), 201; and "From a London paper of June 17," quoted in *Niles' Weekly Register*, September 24, 1814.

2. Mary Stockton Hunter to Susan Stockton Cuthbert, August 30, 1814, Miscellaneous Hunter Manuscripts, New-York Historical Society, quoted in Pitch, *The Burning of Washington*, 124.

3. George Douglass to Henry Wheaton, August 30, 1814, Vertical Files, Fort McHenry National Monument, quoted in Scott S. Sheads, *Fort McHenry* (Baltimore, Md.: The Nautical and Aviation Publishing Company of America, 1995), 30–31.

4. DeWitt Clinton is quoted in Charles G. Muller, *The Darkest Day: The Washington-Baltimore Campaign during the War of 1812* (Philadelphia: University of Pennsylvania Press, 2003), 170–171. James Madison, "Proclamation upon British Depredations—Burning of the Capitol," September 1, 1814, in John Woolley and Gerhard Peters, The American Presidency Project, available online at http://www.presidency.ucsb.edu/ws/?pid=65968.

5. Commodore John Rodgers to William Jones, August 29, 1814, Rodgers Family Papers (Naval Historical Foundation), Library of Congress.

6. A good account of the battle at North Point is found in Whitehorne, *The Battle for Baltimore*, 175–191.

7. Captain Joseph H. Nicholson to James Monroe, September 17, 1814, Nicholson Papers, Library of Congress, quoted in Scott S. Sheads, *Guardian of the Star-Spangled Banner: Lt. Colonel George Armistead and the Fort McHenry Flag* (Baltimore, Md.: Toomey Press, 1999), 18.

8. For a description of the bombardment based on the most recent evidence, see Pitch, *The Burning of Washington*, 197–217; also see Scott S. Sheads, *The Rocket's Red Glare: The Maritime Defense of Baltimore in 1814* (Centerville, Md.: Tidewater, 1986). Midshipman Barrett's description of the flag being raised is in Robert J. Barrett, "Naval Recollections of the Late American War," *United Service Journal* (April 1843): 460; and Private Munroe's is in Scott S. Sheads, "'Yankee Doodle Played': A Letter from Baltimore, 1814," *Maryland Historical Magazine* 76, no. 4 (Winter 1981): 381–382.

9. Virginia Armistead Garber, *The Armistead Family, 1635–1910* (Richmond, Va.: Whittet and Shepperson, 1910), 63; and P. W. Filby and Edward G. Howard, *Star-Spangled Books* (Baltimore: Maryland Historical Society, 1972), 23–24.

10. Sheads, *Guardian of the Star-Spangled Banner*, 21.

11. *Niles' Weekly Register*, May 11, 1816.

12. The source for the inscription is the punchbowl itself. For more on the Armistead presentation silver and portrait, see Margaret Brown Klapthor, "Presentation Pieces in the Museum of History and Technology," *Contributions from the Museum of History and Technology*, Bulletin 241 (Washington, D.C.: Smithsonian Institution, 1965), 85–86; Eleanor McSherry Fowble, "Rembrandt Peale in Baltimore," M.A. thesis, University of Delaware, 1965, 98–106; *Niles' Weekly Register*, May 3, 1818; and Benson J. Lossing, *The Pictorial Field-Book of the War of 1812* (New York: Harper and Bros., 1868), 960.

13. Sheads, *Guardian of the Star-Spangled Banner*, 29–30.

14. Albert Gallatin is quoted in Muller, *The Darkest Day*, 211.

Chapter 1: Sidebar (President Madison's War Message to Congress)

1. Hickey, *The War of 1812*, 44–46.

2. For complete text of President Madison's message to Congress, see *Journal of the House of Representatives of the United States*, vol. 8 (1811–1813): 454–457.

Chapter 1: Sidebar (Dolley Madison's Letter from Washington)

1. See David B. Mattern, "Dolley Madison Has the Last Word: The Famous Letter," *White House History* 4 (Fall 1998): 38–43.

2. Dolley Payne Madison to Anna Cutts, August 23, 1814, Library of Congress, transcription provided by the Dolley Madison Project, available online at http://moderntimes.vcdh.virginia.edu/madison/exhibit/washington/letters/082314.html.

Chapter 1: Sidebar (Lieutenant Colonel George Armistead's Account of the Bombardment of Fort McHenry)

1. This is the text of Armistead's report as published in *Niles' Weekly Register* on October 1, 1814. The emendations in brackets were supplied by Scott Sheads, ranger-historian at Fort McHenry National Monument and Historic Shrine.

Chapter 2: The Song

Epigraph: From the *Baltimore American*, January 13, 1843.

1. These sentiments of Key's are cited in Delaplaine, *Francis Scott Key*, 99–100.

2. Key's letter to his father is reproduced in Filby and Howard, *Star-Spangled Books*, 38 and 151. For more on Key's military service, see Sam Meyer, *Paradoxes of Fame: The Francis Scott Key Story* (Annapolis, Md.: Eastwind Publishing, 1995), 26–28.

3. Key as cited in Meyer, *Paradoxes of Fame*, 9.

4. More than ninety years after the song was written, Oscar Sonneck, chief of the Division of Music at the Library of Congress, undertook a scholarly investigation of its history, in which he attempted to reconcile Taney's and Skinner's accounts with other pieces of evidence about the song. The Library of Congress first published his *Report on "The Star-Spangled Banner," "Hail Columbia," "America," and "Yankee Doodle"* in 1909. Revised in 1914, the book remains one of the standard works on the subject. In 1969, Edward G. Howard and P. W. Filby of the Maryland Historical Society, in the course of producing an exhibition about "The Star-Spangled Banner," reexamined Skinner's and Taney's accounts in the light of additional evidence that had emerged since Sonneck's work was published. Howard and Filby's conclusions were published in the exhibition's catalogue, *Star-Spangled Books*, published by the Maryland Historical Society in 1972. These twentieth-century scholars have enabled modern historians to construct a fairly accurate chronology of the events that led to the writing and publication of Key's poem.

5. Ralph J. Robinson, "New Facts in the National Anthem Story," *Baltimore* 49 (September 1956): 33, 35, 37; and Filby and Howard, *Star-Spangled Books*, 29–33, 42–45.

6. Henry V. D. Jones, ed., *Poems of the Late Francis S. Key, Esq.* (New York: Robert Carter and Bros., 1857), 24–25, 26.

7. *Boston Independent Chronicle*, December 30, 1805; *New York Evening Post*, January 9, 1806; and *Frederick-Town [Maryland] Herald*, January 18, 1806.

8. William Lichtenwanger, *The Music of the Star-Spangled Banner from Ludgate Hill to Capitol Hill* (Washington, D.C.: Library of Congress, 1977), 4–7, 12, 21–24; and Oscar George Theodore Sonneck, *"The Star-Spangled Banner"* (1914, reprint; New York: Da Capo Press, 1969), 15–17.

9. Of the sixty-nine early (1814–1864) printings of "The Star-Spangled Banner" that historians have documented, two-thirds date from after 1851. See Joseph Muller, *The Star-Spangled Banner* (New York: G. A. Baker & Co., 1935); and Lester S. Levy and James J. Fuld, "Unrecorded Early Printings of 'The Star-Spangled Banner,'" *Notes*, 2nd ser., 27, no. 2 (December 1970): 245–251.

10. *Louisville Public Advertiser*, March 20, 1822; *New York Herald*, December 27, 1845; and the *Daily Cleveland Herald*, July 10, 1856.

11. *National Advocate*, November 28, 1817, and November 30, 1818; and the *Cleveland Herald*, July 3, 1851.

12. *New-Hampshire Statesman and State Journal*, December 9, 1837.

13. Meyer, *Paradoxes of Fame*, 29–30.

14. *Emancipator and Free American*, December 10, 1841; and *The North Star*, May 5, 1848.

15. George J. Svejda, *History of the Star-Spangled Banner, 1814 to the Present* (Washington, D.C.: U.S. Department of the Interior, 1969), 113–114, 122–124, 130–131; Sonneck, *The Star-Spangled Banner*, 84–86; *Baltimore American*, January 13, 1843; and *The Ohio Statesman*, November 24, 1841.

16. S. Millett Thompson, *Thirteenth Regiment of New Hampshire Volunteer Infantry in the War of the Rebellion, 1861–1865: A Diary Covering Three Years and a Day* (Boston: Houghton, Mifflin and Company, 1888), 369, quoted in Jon Newsom, "The American Brass Band Movement: A Historical Overview," American Memory, Library of Congress, available online at http://memory.loc.gov/ammem/cwmhtml/cwmpres07.html.

17. Svejda, *History of the Star-Spangled Banner*, 162–219, 222, 232–233, 236, 239–240, 259–260; and Sonneck, *The Star-Spangled Banner*, 82–83.

18. Svejda, *History of the Star-Spangled Banner*, 329–339.

19. Richard S. Hill, "A Proposed Official Version of the Star-Spangled Banner," *Notes*, 2nd ser., 15, no. 1 (December 1957): 33–42.

Chapter 2: Sidebar (Personalizing the Anthem)

1. "Stravinsky's Bit," *Time*, December 22, 1941; "Revised Anthem Played," *New York Times*, January 15, 1944; "Stravinsky Liable to Fine," *New York Times*, January 16, 1944; and "Stravinsky Sticks to True Version of National Anthem," *Chicago Daily Tribune*, January 30, 1944.

2. Feliciano Enterprises, Inc., "José Feliciano: The National Anthem," available online at http://www.josefeliciano.com/anthem .html; and "The Newfangled 'Banner,'" *Entertainment Weekly*, October 11, 1996.

3. Hendrix's comments are featured in *Jimi Hendrix: Live at Woodstock*, DVD, directed by Albert Goodman and Michael Wadleigh, Geffen Records Pty. Ltd., 2005, quoted in Marios Elles, "Chinese Whispers: Jimi Hendrix, Fame, and 'The Star-Spangled Banner,'" *49th Parallel* no. 17 (Spring 2006), available online at http://www.49thparallel.bham.ac.uk/back/issue17/Elles.pdf. For sample critical reactions to Hendrix's rendition of the national anthem, see Craig McGregor, "Woodstock: A Desperate Fear for the Future?" *New York Times*, April 19, 1970; and William C. Woods, "A Fraud-Treasure," *Washington Post, Times Herald*, May 22, 1970; for fans' response, see William E. Farrell, "Nineteen-Hour Concert Ends Bethel Fair," *New York Times*, August 19, 1969.

Meanings and Memories: The Flag in the Civil War

1. Private Sherman is quoted in James McPherson, *For Cause and Comrades: Why Men Fought in the Civil War* (New York: Oxford University Press, 1997), 178. For more on the use and meaning of the American flag in the Civil War, see Scot M. Guenter, *The American Flag, 1777–1924: Cultural Shifts from Creation to Codification* (London and Toronto: Associated University Presses, 1990), 64–87.

Chapter 3: Making the Flag

Epigraph: Robert Barrett, a British veteran of the Battle of Baltimore, described the Star-Spangled Banner as such in his "Naval Recollections," *United Service Journal* (April 1843): 464–465.

1. Armistead's letter is quoted in Walter Lord, *By the Dawn's Early Light* (New York: W. W. Norton, 1972), 274. His request for the Fort Niagara flag is described in Brian Leigh Dunnigan, "Fort Niagara's Star-Spangled Banner: A Garrison Color of the War of 1812," *Military Collector and Historian* 50, no. 2 (Summer 1998): 75–76.

2. Mary-Paulding Martin, *The Flag House Story* (Baltimore, Md.: The Star-Spangled Banner Flag House Association, n.d.), 1–2, 9.

3. Indenture of Grace Wisher to Mary Pickersgill, Baltimore County, Orphans' Court, Indentures, January 6, 1810. The story of Grace Wisher was discovered by T. Stephen Whitman, assistant professor of history at Mount St. Mary's University, while conducting research for the Flag House and Star-Spangled Banner Museum in 2004. His scholarly work includes *The Price of Freedom: Slavery and Manumission in Baltimore and Early National Maryland* (Lexington: University Press of Kentucky, 1997).

4. Official U.S. flags continued to be made with imported bunting until the end of the Civil War, when Congress passed a law requiring the federal government to purchase "Bunting of American manufacture." For more on this topic, see Grace Rogers Cooper, *Thirteen-Star Flags: Keys to Identification* (Washington, D.C.: Smithsonian Institution Press, 1973), 14, 17, 22, 54n.

5. Caroline Pickersgill Purdy to Georgiana Armistead Appleton, undated [1876], Appleton Family Papers, Massachusetts Historical Society, Boston.

6. John H. Rogers is quoted in Muller, *The Darkest Day*, 177.

7. Historian Lossing's insights are discussed in "The Star-Spangled Banner," *The American Historical Record* 2, no. 3 (January 1873): 24.

8. Lord, *By the Dawn's Early Light*, 365.

9. Mendes I. Cohen to George Preble, August 24, 1873, George Henry Preble Papers, American Antiquarian Society, Worcester, Mass.

10. Purdy to Appleton, undated [1876], Appleton Family Papers.

11. *Journals of the Continental Congress*, October 27, 1780, 984; and William Rea Furlong and Byron McCandless, *So Proudly We Hail: The History of the United States Flag* (Washington, D.C.: Smithsonian Institution Press, 1981), 100–101. For more on Hopkinson and his unsuccessful efforts to secure payment for designing the flag, see George Everett Hastings, *The Life and Works of Francis Hopkinson* (New York: Russell & Russell, 1968), 240–254.

12. George Washington to Joseph Reed, January 4, 1776, in John C. Fitzpatrick, ed., *The Writings of George Washington from the Original Manuscript Sources, 1754–1799*, vol. 4 (Washington, D.C.: U.S. Government Printing Office, 1931–1944), 210–211. For more on the Union and Sons of Liberty flags, see Guenter, *The American Flag*, 28–29.

13. *Journals of the Continental Congress*, June 20, 1782, 339. The symbolism of the flag's colors is discussed in Whitney Smith, *The Flag Book of the United States* (New York: William Morrow and Co., Inc., 1975), 87.

14. The changes in the flag's design are described in Furlong and McCandless, *So Proudly We Hail*, 98–101, 115–119, 158.

Chapter 3: Sidebar (What about Betsy Ross?)

1. William J. Canby, "The History of the Flag of the United States," paper read to the Historical Society of Pennsylvania, Philadelphia, 1870, quoted in John B. Harker, *Betsy Ross's Five Pointed Star: Elizabeth Claypoole, Quaker Flag Maker—A Historical Perspective* (Melbourne Beach, Fla.: Canmore Press, 2005), 37–39.

2. For more on the history of the Betsy Ross myth, see Guenter, *The American Flag*, 29–31, 101–103; and Laurel Thatcher Ulrich, "How Betsy Ross Became Famous: Oral Tradition, Nationalism, and the Invention of History," *Common-place* 8, no. 1 (October 2007), available online at http://common-place.org/vol-08/no-01/ulrich.

Meanings and Memories: Flag Rules and Rituals

1. The Barber bill is quoted in George Henry Preble, *History of the Flag of the United States of America* (Boston: A. Williams and Company, 1880), 603. For more on the history of the flag protection movement, see Guenter, *The American Flag*, 133–181, and Robert Justin Goldstein, *Saving Old Glory: The History of the American Flag Desecration Controversy* (Boulder, Colo.: Westview Press, 1996).

Chapter 4: From Family Keepsake to National Treasure

Epigraph: Georgiana Armistead Appleton, in a letter to George Preble, February 18, 1873, Preble Papers.

1. Georgiana Armistead Appleton to George Preble, July 5, 1873, Preble Papers; *New York Herald*, August 4, 1895; *Baltimore Sun*, June 14, 1907; *Boston Herald*, August 31, 1889; and *Annual Report of the Board of Regents of the Smithsonian Institution, 1907* (Washington, D.C.: U.S. Government Printing Office, 1909), 39.

2. *Daily National Intelligencer*, October 12, 1824; *Baltimore American*, October 9, 1824; and "The Civil and Military Arrangements for the Reception of Major General La Fayette in the City of Baltimore," Francis Scott Key Papers, Maryland Historical Society, Baltimore.

3. *North American and Daily Advertiser*, February 9, 1841; *Baltimore Sun*, January 14, 1843; and Young Men's Whig National Convention of Ratification Held in Baltimore City on the Second of May, 1844 (n.p., n.d.), 2, NMAH, Political History Collection, Becker 227739. 1844. A24.

4. *United States' Telegraph*, September 25, 1828.

5. Filby and Howard, *Star-Spangled Books*, 61.

6. *Baltimore American*, September 14, 1839.

7. Delaplaine, *Francis Scott Key*, 477–478.

8. The Gordon family lore comes from Pattie Cook, interview with author [Lonn Taylor], Louisa, Virginia, July 12, 1997.

9. Appleton to Preble, July 5, 1873, Preble Papers; Preble to Appleton, June 30, 1873, Appleton Papers; *Baltimore Sun*, October 13, 1873; and Baltimore City Register of Wills, vol. 30, 166–170.

10. Georgiana Armistead Appleton to George Armistead Appleton, December 30, 1861, Appleton Papers; Garber, *The Armistead Family*, 71–72; and *Baltimore Sun*, September 9, 1861.

11. *New York Herald*, August 4, 1895.

12. Georgiana Armistead Appleton to George Preble, June 17, 1873, Preble Papers.

13. *The American Historical Record* 2, no. 13 (January 1873): 24.

14. Appleton to Preble, February 18, 1873, Preble Papers.

15. Preble to Appleton, February 26, 1873, March 13, 1873, and June 22, 1873, Appleton Papers; Appleton to Preble, March 8, 1873, Preble Papers; and George H. Preble, *Three Historic Flags and Three September Victories* (Boston: n.p., 1873), 21–22.

16. From the Appleton Papers: Preble to Appleton, August 21, 1873, and December 1, 1874; James Lick to Appleton, January 4, 1874; and Stephen Salisbury to Appleton, June 3, 1874. Salisbury to Preble, September 14, 1873, Preble Papers.

17. From the Appleton Papers: Charles B. Norton to Appleton, March 27, 1873; Alice Etting to Appleton, December 29, 1873; Appleton to Etting (draft), January 18, 1874; and Preble to Appleton, October 6, 1875.

18. Preble to Appleton, July 27, 1876, and August 14, 1876, Appleton Papers; Appleton to Preble, September 9, 1876, Preble Papers.

19. N. Appleton to G. Appleton, November 2, 1875, Appleton Papers.

20. Nathan Appleton, *The Star Spangled Banner* (Boston: Lockwood, Brooks, and Co., 1877), 3–4, 33–34; and *New York Herald*, June 16, 1877.

21. Appleton to Preble, July 5, 1873, Preble Papers.

22. Georgiana Armistead Appleton to Nathan Appleton, April 15, 1861; and William Stuart Appleton to Nathan Appleton, April 6, 1861, Appleton Papers.

23. Appleton to Preble, July 16, 1873, Preble Papers. The other reference to Georgiana Appleton's financial difficulties is from Appleton to Preble, April 27, 1876, Preble Papers.

24. Eben Appleton to Preble, March 15, 1879, Preble Papers.

25. *Baltimore Sun*, October 14, 1880.

26. *Baltimore American*, September 2, 1889.

27. General Macfeely's letter to Eben Appleton appears in the *Baltimore American*, August 29, 1889; Appleton's response appears in the *New York Mail and Express*, August 30, 1889, and the *Baltimore American*, August 31, 1889.

28. *Baltimore American*, September 3, 1889.

29. For a detailed account of the conflict between Eben Appleton and the Baltimore committee over the loan of the Star-Spangled Banner, see the series of articles published in the *Baltimore American*, August 29 through September 3, 1889.

30. Georgiana Appleton Hunter's comments are reported in the *New York Sun*, April 7, 1907. The replica flag presented by Adah Schley is described in the *Baltimore American*, August 29 and September 8, 1889.

Chapter 4: Sidebar (Pieces of History)

1. Quoted in Steven Lubar and Kathleen M. Kendrick, *Legacies: Collecting America's History at the Smithsonian* (Washington, D.C.: Smithsonian Institution Press, 2001), 40. This book includes a detailed discussion of relics in the NMAH collections, including the Star-Spangled Banner; see especially pages 36–47.

Chapter 5: The Star-Spangled Banner Comes to the Smithsonian

Epigraph: Eben Appleton, in a letter to Smithsonian Secretary Charles Walcott, December 12, 1912, Accession File 54876, NMAH, Washington, D.C.

1. Appleton to Walcott, January 10, 1914, Accession File 54876.
2. Smithsonian Institution, *Guidebook to the National Museum* (Washington, D.C.: Smithsonian Institution, 1886). For more information about the "Cabinet of Curiosities," the founding of the Smithsonian Institution, and the establishment of the U.S. National Museum, see Lubar and Kendrick, *Legacies*; James Conaway, *The Smithsonian: 150 Years of Adventure, Discovery, and Wonder* (Washington, D.C.: Smithsonian Institution Press, 1995); and Pamela M. Henson, "Spencer F. Baird's Vision for a National Museum," available online at http://www.siarchives.si.edu/history/exhibits/baird/bairdhm.htm.
3. *Baltimore Sun*, June 30, 1907; and *Baltimore American*, July 10, 1907. From Accession File 54876: Baylor to Walcott, May 29, 1907; Appleton to Baylor, May 24, 1907; Walcott to Baylor, June 4, 1907; Appleton to Walcott, June 11, 1907; Walcott to Appleton, June 19, 1907; Appleton to Walcott, June 25, 1907; Rathbun to Appleton, July 8, 1907; and Rathbun to Appleton, July 11, 1907.
4. From Accession File 54876: Walcott to Rathbun, December 19, 1913; Rathbun to Walcott, December 22, 1913; Walcott to Bibbins, December 29, 1913; Appleton to Walcott, January 5, 1914; Walcott to Appleton, January 8, 1914; Appleton to Walcott, January 10, 1914.
5. From Accession File 54876: Bibbins to Walcott, January 26, 1914; Bibbins to Walcott, June 27, 1914; Bibbins to Walcott, July 1, 1914; and Appleton to Walcott, August 31, 1914. *National Star-Spangled Banner Centennial, Baltimore, Maryland, September 6 to 13, 1914* (Baltimore, Md.: National Star-Spangled Banner Centennial Commission, 1914), 111.
6. Georgiana Armistead Appleton to Preble, March 8, 1873, Preble Papers.
7. Belote to J. E. Holmes, February 3, 1914, Accession File 54876.
8. Holmes to Rathbun, February 10, 1914; Isabel Rives to William Ravenel, March 10, 1914; and Rathbun to Fowler, March 25, 1914.
9. Belote to Holmes, February 3, 1914, Accession File 54876; Sue Lenthe, "Don't Give Up the Flags: The Preservation Efforts of Amelia Bold Fowler and Katherine Fowler Richey," *Piecework* 3, no. 4 (July–August 1995): 60–64; and U.S. Patent No. 1,075,206, issued Octo-ber 7, 1913.
10. Amelia Fowler's Statement Regarding the Star-Spangled Banner, Amelia Fowler Papers, Box I, Folder 18, Massachusetts State Archives, Boston.
11. Mary E. Ludenig, "Saving the Star-Spangled Banner," *St. Nicholas Magazine* 59, no. 9 (July 1932): 464. From Accession File 54876:

Samuel Davis to William Ravenel, April 10, 1914; William Ravenel to Amelia Fowler, May 6, 1914; and Theodore Belote to J. E. Graf, January 18, 1940.
12. Except for the two years between November 1942 and November 1944, when the Star-Spangled Banner was sent to a government warehouse in Shenandoah National Park near Luray, Virginia, to protect it from possible bombing raids.
13. Carmichael as quoted in Smithsonian Institution, *A New Museum of History and Technology for the Smithsonian Institution*, 3. There is no date indicated in the publication, but it seems likely that the brochure was published in the early 1950s to persuade Congress to provide funding for the new Museum of History and Technology.
14. Silvio A. Bedini, "Oddly Enough," internal document, Smithsonian Institution, January 1980, 3.
15. Smithsonian Institution, *A New Museum of History and Technology for the Smithsonian Institution*, 5.
16. Ibid., 14–16.
17. Smithsonian Institution, *The Making of a Modern Museum: Report on the Design and Construction of the National Museum of American History, Behring Center, Second Edition*, internal document, Office of Facilities, Engineering, and Operations, Smithsonian Institution, 2005, 22.

Chapter 5: Sidebar (Hidden Treasure)

1. Appleton to Walcott, August 31, 1914, Accession File 54876.
2. For information relating to the removal of Smithsonian treasures to Luray during World War II, see the Star-Spangled Banner Preservation Project files (hereafter, SSB Project files), Star-Spangled Banner at Luray, Virginia; *Annual Report of the Board of Regents of the Smithsonian Institution, 1945* (Washington, D.C.: Government Printing Office, 1946), 10; "Smithsonian Hid Treasures Near Luray during War," *Washington Post*, October 9, 1946, 2; Rebecca Maksel, "In the Event of War, How the Smithsonian Protected Its 'Strange Animals, Curious Creatures' and More," *Smithsonian Magazine* (May 2007), available online at http://www.smithsonian.com; and Conaway, *The Smithsonian*.

Chapter 6: Centerpiece of a New Museum

Epigraph: Smithsonian Secretary Leonard Carmichael's statement is from Smithsonian Institution, *A New Museum of History and Technology for the Smithsonian Institution*, 5.

1. Senate Report 301, 86th Congress, First Session, May 20, 1959, quoted in *Annual Report of the United States National Museum* (Washington, D.C.: Smithsonian Institution, 1959), 2.

2. Kellogg as quoted in Smithsonian Institution, *A New Museum of History and Technology for the Smithsonian Institution*, 26.

3. "Checklist and Outline of Requirements for the Design of the Museum of History and Technology," revised March 12, 1956, 3. Smithsonian Institution Archives (SIA), RU 50, Box 78, Washington, D.C.

4. Ibid., 6–8, 17.

5. Ibid., 19–20, 24.

6. Smithsonian Institution, *The Making of a Modern Museum*.

7. Edgar M. Howell to Frank Taylor, August 16, 1961, Accession File 54876; William E. Boyle to Howell, November 29, 1963, Folder 13, Star-Spangled Banner File, Textile Collection, NMAH; and Interview, Lonn Taylor with Donald Kloster, August 16, 1999.

8. *Washington Post*, January 23, 1964, A18; *The Evening Star* (Washington, D.C.), May 25, 1962.

Meanings and Memories: The Flag in the Sixties

1. Abbie Hoffman is quoted in Jonah Raskin, *For the Hell of It: The Life and Times of Abbie Hoffman* (Berkeley: University of California Press, 1996), 179.

Chapter 7: Saving the Star-Spangled Banner

Epigraph: Interview with Suzanne Thomassen-Krauss, chief conservator of the SSB Project, True Aim Productions, Inc., April 28, 2003, transcript in SSB Project files, NMAH.

1. Rita J. Adrosko, "Report on the Star-Spangled Banner Conservation Project, December 9, 1981," Accession File 54876; and Paul R. Jett, "The Cleaning and Examination of the Star-Spangled Banner: A Report Submitted to the Division of Conservation, September 29, 1982," Accession File 54876.

2. NMAH, SSB Project, *Star-Spangled Banner Preservation Conference, National Museum of American History, November 22–23, 1996*, SSB Project files, "Conference Summary" folder.

3. Ibid., 2.

4. Ibid., 2–3.

5. Ibid., especially 16–18.

6. Ibid., 2–3.

7. Internal memo, Lucy Greene to Ron Becker, February 5, 1997, SSB Project files.

8. "Smithsonian's Star-Spangled Banner Conservation Laboratory and Exhibition Open at the National Museum of American History," press release, updated August 2, 1999, Office of Public Affairs, NMAH. See also NMAH, *"The Star-Spangled Banner State of the Flag Report,"* internal document, 2001.

9. NMAH, *"The Star-Spangled Banner State of the Flag Report."* See also Paula Johnson and Marilyn Zoidis to Lonnie Bunch, "Recommendation to Proceed with Phase I of Proposed Treatment for the Star-Spangled Banner," June 10, 1999, internal memo, NMAH, SSB Project files, "Treatment Plan—Phase I Comments" folder.

10. SSB Project, "Review of Comments Received on Treatment Proposal, Phase I," August 11, 1999, SSB Project files, "Treatment Plan—Phase I Comments" folder.

11. Research tests were performed by Fenella G. France, Ph.D., research scientist and consultant to the SSB Project.

Chapter 8: A New Home for an Enduring Icon

Epigraph: President William J. Clinton, launching the Save America's Treasures campaign at NMAH, July 13, 1998.

1. Report of the Blue Ribbon Commission, March 2002, Section I. "Transmittal and Summary of Report," Smithsonian Institution, Washington, D.C.

2. Ibid., Section II-B, "The Problem."

3. Ibid.

4. Ibid., Section III-A, "Perspective on the Problems and Their Solution."

5. The original building featured large windows offering wonderful vistas of the Mall and the major monuments. As more and more objects were placed in public corridors and lobby areas, these windows were later blocked to protect objects from exposure to damaging light.

6. Ibid., Section III-B, "Recommendations to Improve the Architectural and Aesthetic Setting for NMAH Exhibits."

7. NMAH, Press Release, "Museum Announces Major Renovation Including New Gallery for Star-Spangled Banner," April 12, 2006, available online at http://americanhistory.si.edu/news/pressrelease.cfm?key=29&newskey=345.

8. Ibid.

9. "Remarks by the President at National Treasures Tour Kick-Off," NMAH, July 13, 1998.

ACKNOWLEDGMENTS

The first three chapters of this book bring together in one place the scholarship of authors who over the past century have probed the story of the flag and the anthem in publications ranging from government reports to books written for popular audiences. Our debts to these authors are acknowledged, at least in part, in the notes at the back of this book. The fourth and fifth chapters present material that is largely the result of research in the George Henry Preble Papers at the American Antiquarian Society in Worcester, Massachusetts; the Appleton Family Papers at the Massachusetts Historical Society in Boston; the Enoch Pratt Free Library and the Maryland Historical Society in Baltimore, Maryland; and the archives of the Smithsonian Institution. The concluding chapters on the Star-Spangled Banner Preservation Project and the construction and renovation of the National Museum of American History draw substantially from the Star-Spangled Banner Preservation Project's archives as well as interviews with staff members who shaped and participated in those efforts.

For guidance and assistance in conducting this research, the authors would first like to thank Scott Sheads and Anna von Lunz of the Fort McHenry National Monument and Historic Shrine. They have been valued collaborators from the very beginning of this project. Sally Johnston and Pat Pilling of the Flag House and Star-Spangled Banner Museum, Joan B. Chaison and Thomas Knoles of the American Antiquarian Society, Peter Drummey of the Massachusetts Historical Society, and Pamela Henson of the Smithsonian Institution Archives have also rendered invaluable assistance.

At the National Museum of American History we gratefully acknowledge our past and present colleagues on the Star-Spangled Banner Presrvation Project team who contributed to the development of this book, including Hal Aber, Ron Becker, Carol Frost, Jim Gardner, La Tasha Harris, Valeska Hilbig, Suzanne Thomassen-Krauss, Amy Venzke, and Marilyn Zoidis. Many other Smithsonian colleagues—including Rita Adrosko, Doris Bowman, Lonnie Bunch, Kathy Dirks, Jennifer Jones, Donald Kloster, and Susan Myers—provided useful information and thoughtful feedback at various stages of the project. Randy Inouye and Patrick Ladden supplied critical information and insight about the renovation project. Interns Jenna Andrews, Susan Clark, and Sascha Scott provided research assistance and helped solve several historical puzzles. Martha Davidson and Laura McClure helped track down elusive photographs and obtained permission for their use in this book. David Miller provided generous assistance with artifact and graphic research, and Stevan Fisher graciously lent his design expertise.

For providing us with so many wonderful illustrations, we are indebted to the photographers and staff of Smithsonian Photographic Services, including Michael Barnes, David Burgevin, John Dillaber, Harold Dorwin, Dane Penland, Richard Strauss, Hugh Talman, and Jeff Tinsley. Through their skill, dedication, and artistry, they have helped to create and maintain a visual record of the Star-Spangled Banner at the Smithsonian.

We especially would like to thank the members of the Armistead family who have shared material and memories, including George Armistead III, Henry Armistead, Robert Bradford, Tom and Beverly Gordon, Christopher Morton, Edwin Morton, and Theodore Morton.

We would also like to thank Caroline Newman, our editor at Smithsonian Books, for her guidance and expertise; the creative staff at Marquand Books for producing such a beautifully designed publication; and copyeditor Amy Smith Bell for her patient and skillful work on the text.

Finally, we would like to express our appreciation to Ralph Lauren for contributing the foreword to the book, and also for the inspiring and generous support he has given to the Star-Spangled Banner Preservation Project.

INDEX

PHOTO CREDITS

American Antiquarian Society, Worcester, Mass.: 80

AP / Wide World Photos: 133 (lower left)

© Bettmann / CORBIS: 6, 132, 133 (lower right)

Anne S. K. Brown Military Collection, Brown University Library: 70

The John Carter Brown Library at Brown University: 72

Conway Library, Courtauld Institute of Art: 45

© Henry Diltz / CORBIS: 49 (right)

Duke University, Rare Book, Manuscript, and Special Collections
Library: 60 (upper right)

The Flag House and Star-Spangled Banner Museum, Baltimore, Md.:
66, 67 (left)

The Granger Collection, New York: 17

© 1976 Matt Herron / Take Stock: 133 (top)

© Brooks Kraft / CORBIS: 8

Library of Congress: 20 (top), 26 (left), 33, 38, 49 (left), 53, 54, 73,
79 (top and lower left), 88 (left), 117 (right), 119

Maryland Historical Society, Baltimore, Md.: 21 (left and right), 22,
41 (left), 43, 55, 88 (right), 99 (right), 100

© Michael Mauney / Time & Life Pictures / Getty Images: 49 (center)

Minneapolis Institute of Arts, The William Hood Dunwoody Fund:
74 (right)

Christopher Hughes Morton: 87, 99 (left)

NASA, Johnson Space Center Digital Image Collection: 130 (left)

National Archives and Records Administration: 10, 74 (left),
118 (lower right), 121

The National Park Service, Fort McHenry National Monument
and Historic Shrine: 23, 83 (right)

New York Public Library, Schomburg Center for Research in Black
Culture: 51

Peabody Essex Museum, Salem, Mass.: 89

Pennsylvania Academy of Fine Arts, Philadelphia (Archives):
61 (top)

Pennsylvania State Archives: 69

Pickersgill Retirement Community, Towson, Md.: 65

© 2001 The Record (Bergen County, N.J.): 7

© Chuck Savage / CORBIS: 57

B. Anthony Stewart / NGS Image Collection: 111

U.S. Naval Academy Museum: 12

U.S. Patent and Trademark Office: 108 (left)

The Walters Art Museum, Baltimore, Md.: 41 (right)

White House Historical Association (White House Collection): 15, 19

Wisconsin Historical Society, WHi-5348: 4 (right)

O say can you see

what so proudly we hail'd

hose broad stripes & bright st

'er the ramparts we watch

And the rocket's red

gave proof through the

O say does that star spang

O'er the land of the free

On the shore dimly seen

Where the foe's haughty

What is that which the

As it fitfully blows, half

Now it catches the g